# Hi Ho, Hi Ho, It's off to Work we go!

Generally tickets show the journey to be made but not the reason for that journey. H
their appearance or the text on the ticket give a clue to the reason behind the journey.
into some of the tickets devised for a wide range of working environments and how some might have been affected by national or even international events.

My father went to work by train from Forest Hill to London Bridge station and then walked across London Bridge to his office in Cornhill. The Southern Railway had its own way of doing things. One of the features of Southern Railway season tickets, and some other types of tickets, was the use of red ink in the pad for stamping the weekly code on weekly tickets and sometimes also the expiry date.

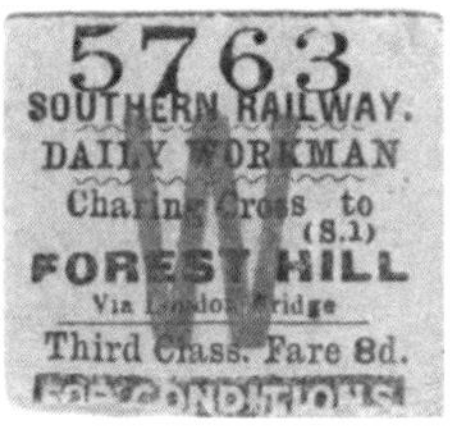


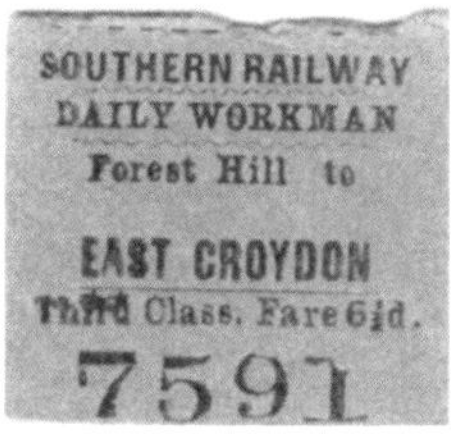


Their season tickets were larger than most railways and most return tickets were printed vertically, but they did adhere to grey as the colour of Workmans' tickets.

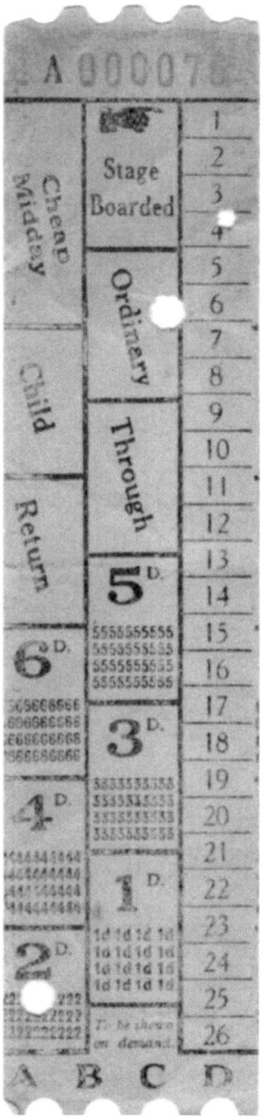

In the winter the wind and rain make walking across London Bridge unpleasant, to say the least. Many of the commuters arriving at London Bridge station opted to catch a bus across the bridge. This gave the conductors a problem; how to collect fares from all the passengers before they got off on the far side of the bridge and disappeared into their offices. There were a few trials of ticket machines but none of these produced an acceptable solution to the problem. In June 1927 (ticket dated 26.5.29) the L.G.O.C. had tried an A.C. Aspinall machine which issued tickets by pressing buttons which punched holes to record the fare, type of fare and the stage boarded. These details were recorded in the machine, thus saving the use of a waybill. Not much use in speeding up fare collection and ticket issue!

This ticket is believed to have been issued in 1930 through a Hall ticket machine. It has provision for a date of issue, counting the days from 1st January, Stage Boarded, Route and Class, across the ticket while the fare paid is shown in the top left hand corner.

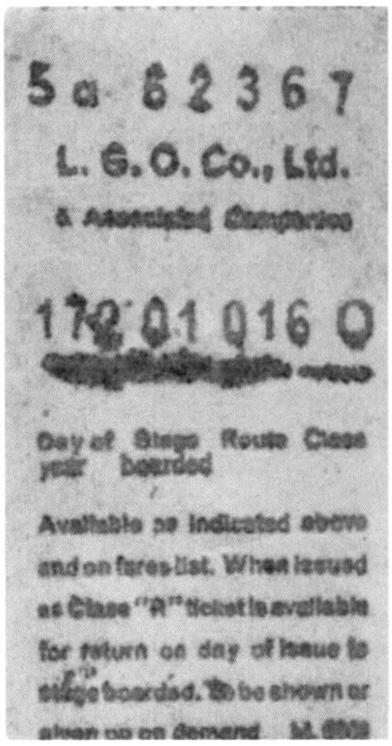


Some TIM machines were used, but not on a large scale. That with the red ink is dated 1939 while the mauve printed one is from 1954. TIMs were used by queue conductors and this one shows the issuing point as being London Bridge.

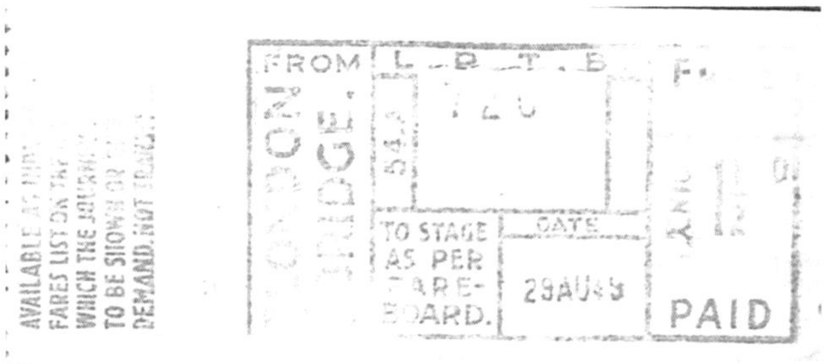

When mechanisation came in force to London's buses in the 1950's, it was with Gibson ticket machines. A large number of railway Early Morning Returns were abolished from 1st November 1959, which just left Early Morning Single tickets.

Briefly back to Forest Hill with punch Workmen's returns from the routes through Forest Hill in the period when punch tickets still held sway. It is difficult to realise that 2d was sufficient to buy a return ticket especially considering such extensive transfer opportunities, such as on these examples.

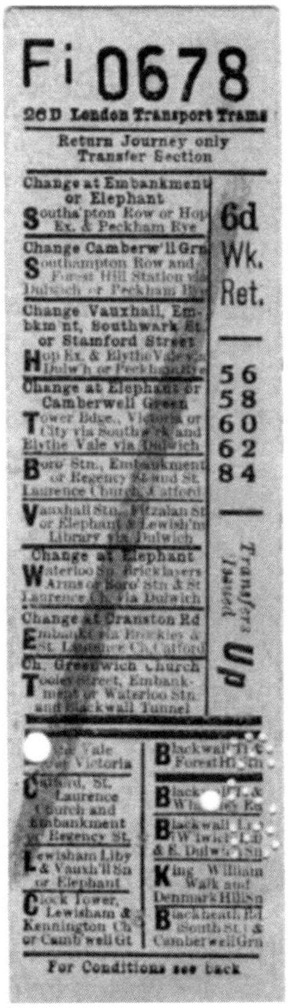


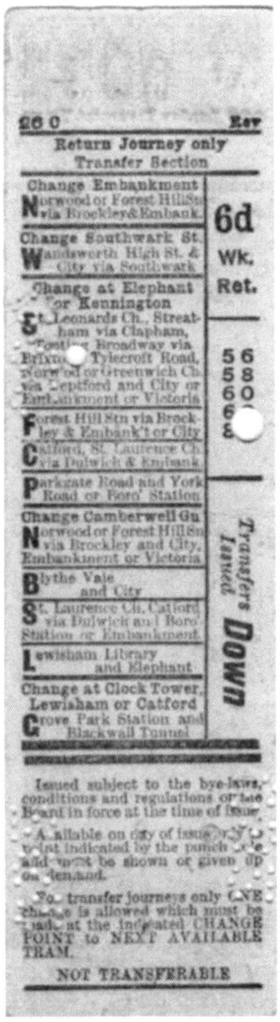


The Workmen's returns are quite long, but the front is insufficient to carry all the information and needs lengthy provisions on the back. The pinholes from the conductor's clippers are visible on this example.

The 2nd World War was still being fought when I was born so I have to rely on contemporary reports detailing the part that the railways played in both the 1st and 2nd World Wars, and as here even the Boer War. Special platform tickets were produced to allow families to see their relative off on the special troop trains on the first leg of their journey to the front.

Tuesday, February 12, 1901.
2nd Vol. Batt. Prince of Wales's North Staff. Regiment.
Volunteers for the Front.
PASS BEARER
To Platform, to see Relative off to Lichfield by Special 3-10 p.m.
WILLIAM WALTERS.
BURTON-ON-TRENT.
You MUST be on the Platform before Quarter to Three.

A page from a Combined Leave and Railway ticket from 1918 covering the journey from France to Devon. Combined Leave and Railway Tickets were produced in booklets with individual pages for the various stages in the journey from, and back to their regiment. On this ticket from 1918 the starting point is just "FRANCE" and travel was provided on the railways in Great Britain and Ireland (including the Underground Railways) and on the Steamers running to and from the ports. Being in uniform is only mentioned at the top of the ticket.

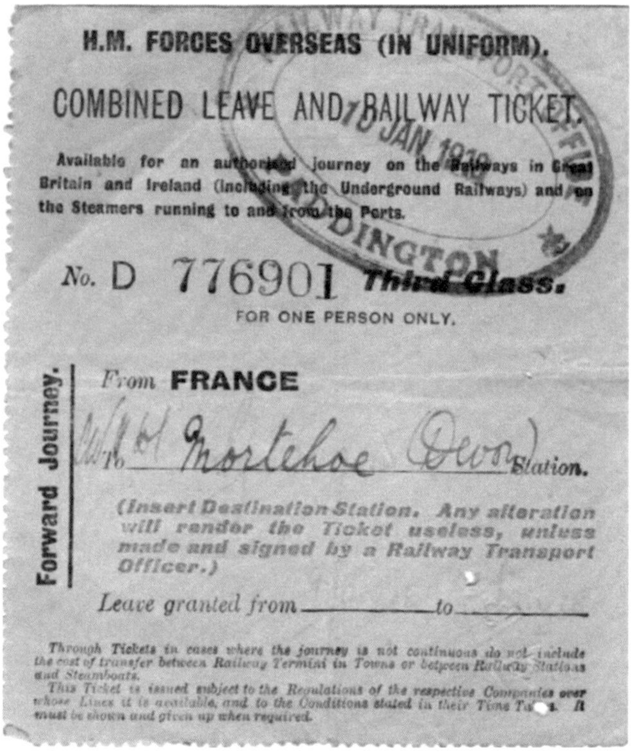
H.M. FORCES OVERSEAS (IN UNIFORM).

COMBINED LEAVE AND RAILWAY TICKET.

Available for an authorised journey on the Railways in Great Britain and Ireland (including the Underground Railways) and on the Steamers running to and from the Ports.

No. D 776901 Third Class.

FOR ONE PERSON ONLY.

Forward Journey.

From FRANCE

W.H. To Mortehoe (Devon) Station.

(Insert Destination Station. Any alteration will render the Ticket useless, unless made and signed by a Railway Transport Officer.)

Leave granted from ______ to ______

Through Tickets in cases where the journey is not continuous do not include the cost of transfer between Railway Termini in Towns or between Railway Stations and Steamboats.

This Ticket is issued subject to the Regulations of the respective Companies over whose Lines it is available, and to the Conditions stated in their Time Tables. It must be shown and given up when required.

Wearing or not wearing uniform has been a contentious subject for many past years. During "The Troubles" in Northern Island being in uniform in public was dangerous. Only last year the Woolwich murder gave rise to a restriction on wearing military or civilian clothes that suggested a connection with the forces in public, although this lasted only a day or two.

This is one of two further Combined Leave and Railway tickets booklets, this time from World War II. By the Government of Ireland Act of 1920 Northern Ireland was created together with what was then Southern Ireland. Partition was reinforced in 1923 when what was to be Southern Ireland separated from the United Kingdom.

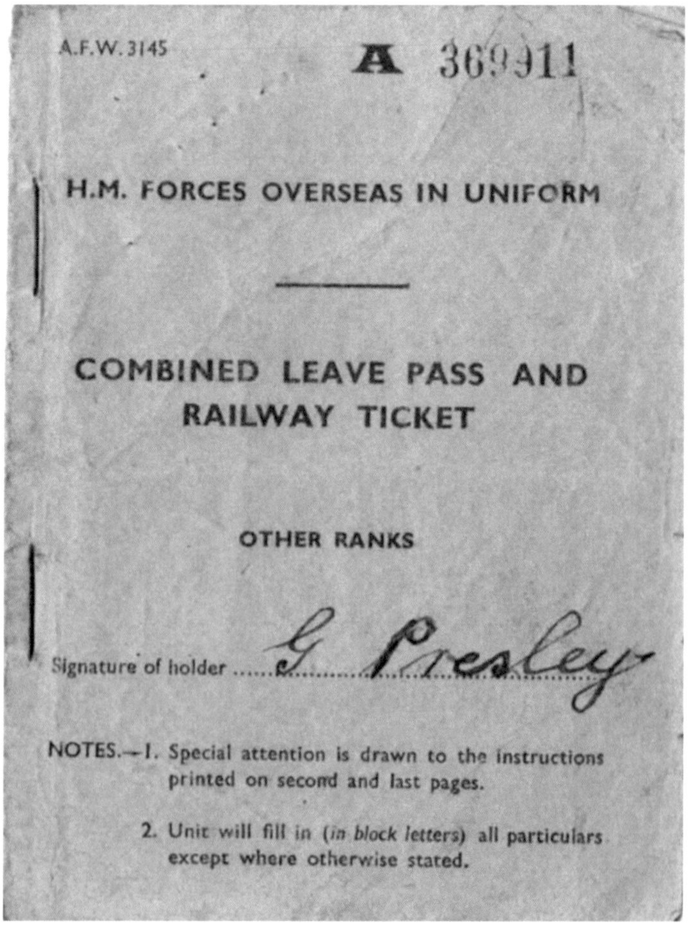
A.F.W. 3145

A 369911

H.M. FORCES OVERSEAS IN UNIFORM

COMBINED LEAVE PASS AND RAILWAY TICKET

OTHER RANKS

Signature of holder ........G. Presley

NOTES.—1. Special attention is drawn to the instructions printed on second and last pages.

2. Unit will fill in (*in block letters*) all particulars except where otherwise stated.

The top line of the second page requires soldiers on leave to be properly dressed in uniform when in public except that plain clothes may be worn for the purpose of athletic exercise for which a special dress was necessary.

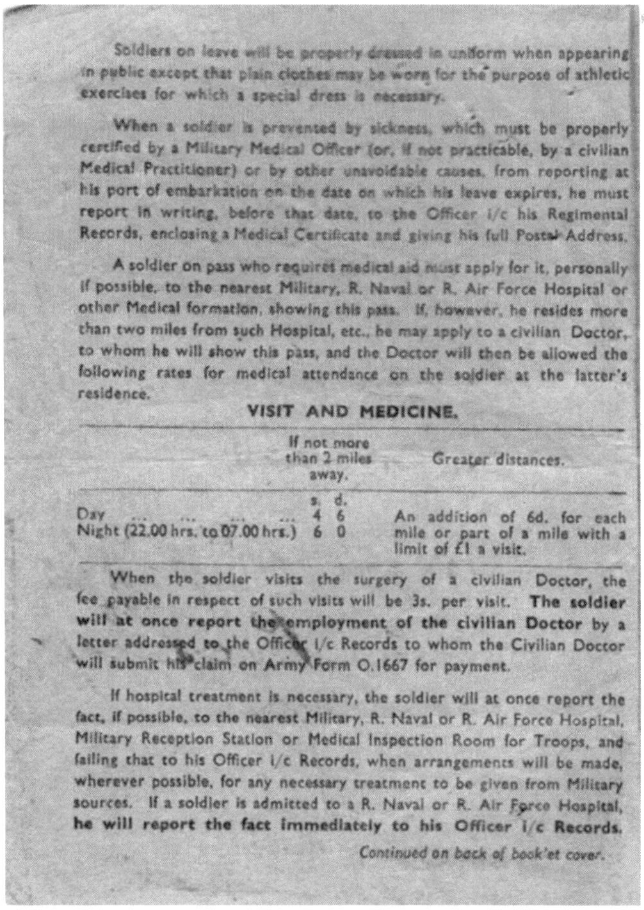

Soldiers on leave will be properly dressed in uniform when appearing in public except that plain clothes may be worn for the purpose of athletic exercises for which a special dress is necessary.

When a soldier is prevented by sickness, which must be properly certified by a Military Medical Officer (or, if not practicable, by a civilian Medical Practitioner) or by other unavoidable causes, from reporting at his port of embarkation on the date on which his leave expires, he must report in writing, before that date, to the Officer i/c his Regimental Records, enclosing a Medical Certificate and giving his full Postal Address.

A soldier on pass who requires medical aid must apply for it, personally if possible, to the nearest Military, R. Naval or R. Air Force Hospital or other Medical formation, showing this pass. If, however, he resides more than two miles from such Hospital, etc., he may apply to a civilian Doctor, to whom he will show this pass, and the Doctor will then be allowed the following rates for medical attendance on the soldier at the latter's residence.

**VISIT AND MEDICINE.**

| | If not more than 2 miles away. | Greater distances. |
|---|---|---|
| | s. d. | |
| Day ... ... ... ... | 4 6 | An addition of 6d. for each mile or part of a mile with a limit of £1 a visit. |
| Night (22.00 hrs. to 07.00 hrs.) | 6 0 | |

When the soldier visits the surgery of a civilian Doctor, the fee payable in respect of such visits will be 3s. per visit. **The soldier will at once report the employment of the civilian Doctor** by a letter addressed to the Officer i/c Records to whom the Civilian Doctor will submit his claim on Army Form O.1667 for payment.

If hospital treatment is necessary, the soldier will at once report the fact, if possible, to the nearest Military, R. Naval or R. Air Force Hospital, Military Reception Station or Medical Inspection Room for Troops, and failing that to his Officer i/c Records, when arrangements will be made, wherever possible, for any necessary treatment to be given from Military sources. If a soldier is admitted to a R. Naval or R. Air Force Hospital, **he will report the fact immediately to his Officer i/c Records.**

*Continued on back of booklet cover.*

The method of transport is similar in layout to the World War I pass except it takes note of the position of Eire, which was neutral during WW II, and the availability is set out in detail being the Railways in Great Britain, including London Transport Railways; also for a journey by steamboat in Scotland, from stations and ports in Northern Ireland (not via Dublin or other ports in Eire), and still included the Channel Islands, Isle of Wight, and Isle of Man.

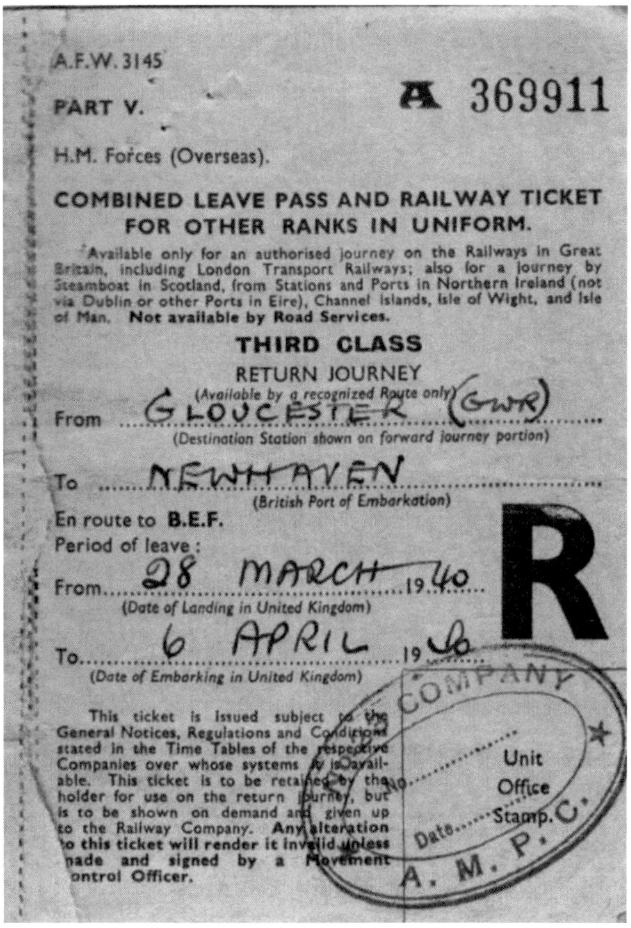

A.F.W. 3145

**PART V.** **A 369911**

H.M. Forces (Overseas).

**COMBINED LEAVE PASS AND RAILWAY TICKET FOR OTHER RANKS IN UNIFORM.**

Available only for an authorised journey on the Railways in Great Britain, including London Transport Railways; also for a journey by Steamboat in Scotland, (from Stations and Ports in Northern Ireland (not via Dublin or other Ports in Eire), Channel Islands, Isle of Wight, and Isle of Man. **Not available by Road Services.**

**THIRD CLASS**

RETURN JOURNEY

*(Available by a recognized Route only)*

From GLOUCESTER (GWR)

*(Destination Station shown on forward journey portion)*

To NEWHAVEN

*(British Port of Embarkation)*

En route to **B.E.F.**

Period of leave:

From 28 MARCH 1940

*(Date of Landing in United Kingdom)*

To 6 APRIL 1940

*(Date of Embarking in United Kingdom)*

**R**

This ticket is issued subject to the General Notices, Regulations and Conditions stated in the Time Tables of the respective Companies over whose systems it is available. This ticket is to be retained by the holder for use on the return journey, but is to be shown on demand and given up to the Railway Company. **Any alteration to this ticket will render it invalid unless made and signed by a Movement Control Officer.**

Unit Office Stamp.

Date

COMPANY A. M. P. C.

The next coupon is the Leave Embarkation Card for the return journey.

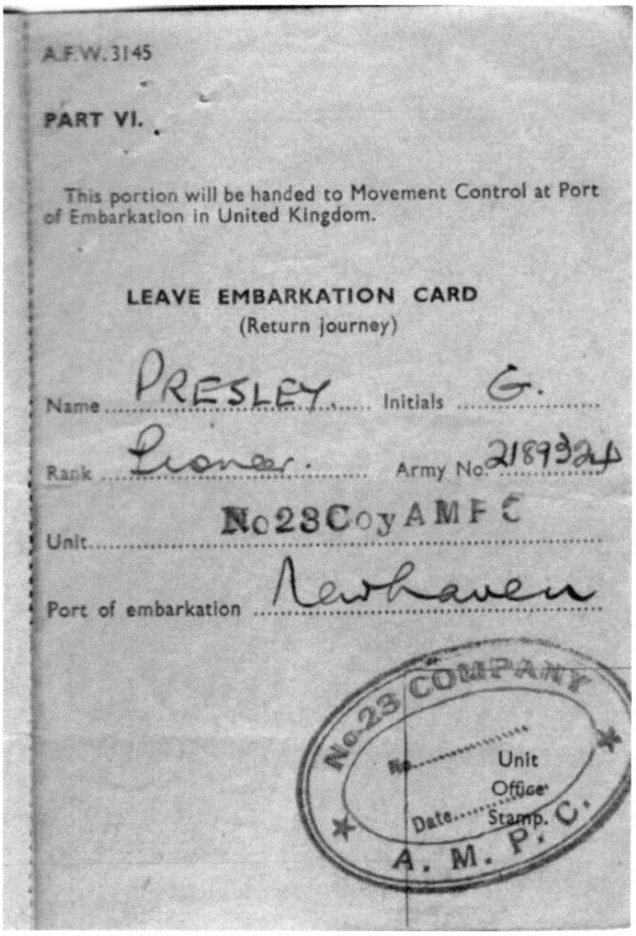

A.F.W. 3145

PART VI.

This portion will be handed to Movement Control at Port of Embarkation in United Kingdom.

LEAVE EMBARKATION CARD
(Return journey)

Name PRESLEY. Initials G.

Rank Pioneer. Army No. 2189324

Unit No23CoyAMPC

Port of embarkation Newhaven

No23 COMPANY A.M.P.C. No. ... Unit Office Date ... Stamp.

For some reason this coupon was not handed in on re-joining his unit

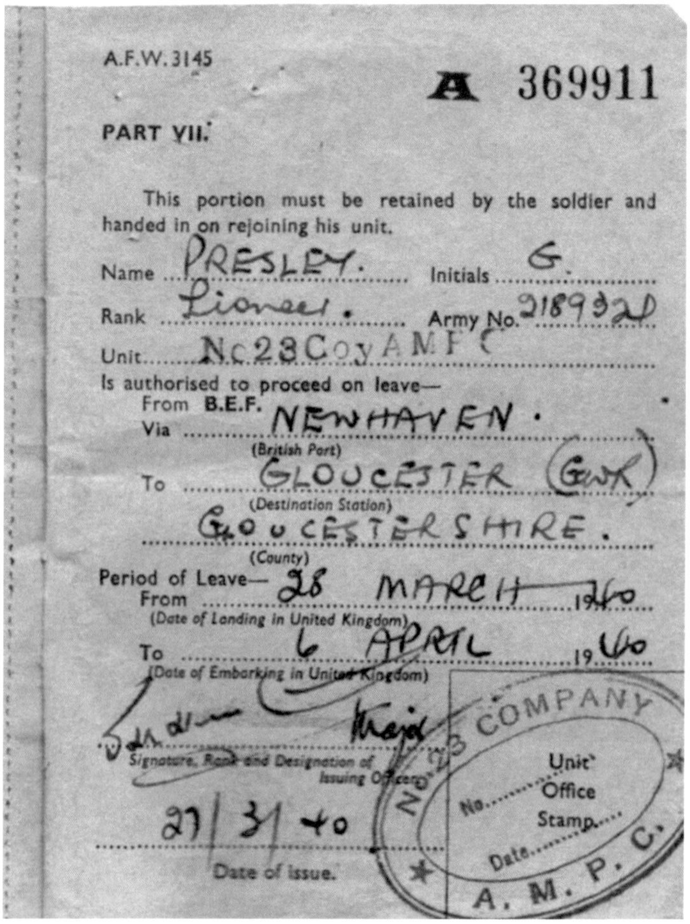

A.F.W. 3145

**A** 369911

PART VII.

This portion must be retained by the soldier and handed in on rejoining his unit.

Name PRESLEY. Initials G.

Rank Pioneer. Army No. 2189324

Unit No23CoyAMPC

Is authorised to proceed on leave—
From B.E.F.
Via NEWHAVEN.
(British Port)
To GLOUCESTER (GWR)
(Destination Station)
GLOUCESTERSHIRE.
(County)

Period of Leave—
From 28 MARCH 1940
(Date of Landing in United Kingdom)
To 6 APRIL 1940
(Date of Embarking in United Kingdom)

Major
Signature, Rank and Designation of Issuing Officer.

27/3/40
Date of issue.

No23 COMPANY A.M.P.C. No. ... Unit Office Stamp. Date ...

We now come to the Army Expeditionary Force booklet which does not have any mention of uniform on the front cover but does draw special attention to the instructions printed on the second page. The stamps on this pass show that both arrival and departure were via the port of Folkestone.

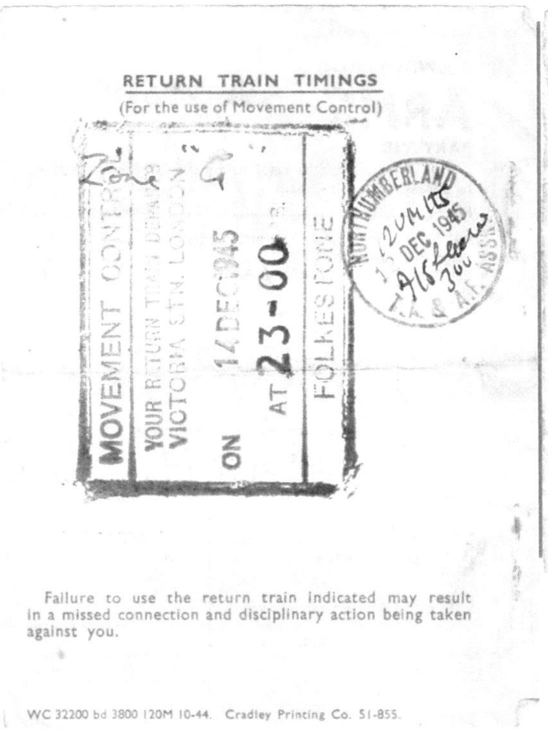
RETURN TRAIN TIMINGS
(For the use of Movement Control)

MOVEMENT CONTROL
YOUR RETURN TRAIN DEPARTS
VICTORIA STN. LONDON
ON 14 DEC 1945
AT 23-00
FOLKESTONE

Failure to use the return train indicated may result in a missed connection and disciplinary action being taken against you.

WC 32200 bd 3800 120M 10-44. Cradley Printing Co. 51-855.

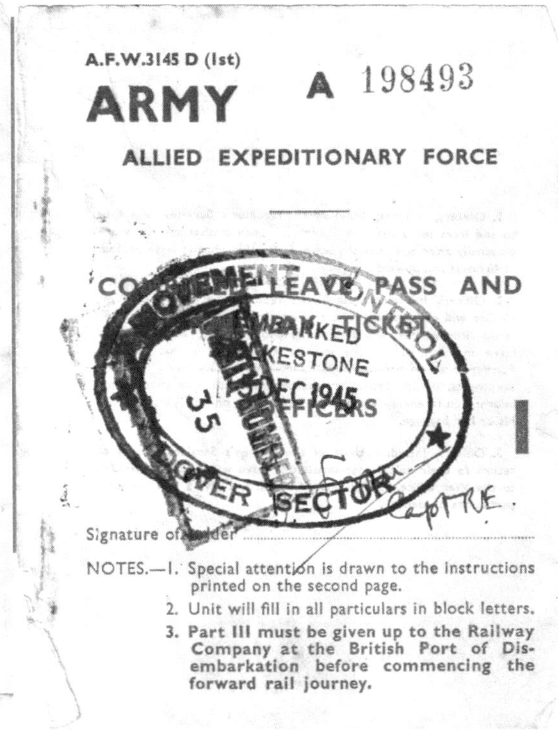
A.F.W.3145 D (Ist)

ARMY A 198493

ALLIED EXPEDITIONARY FORCE

CONTINENTAL LEAVE PASS AND

Signature of holder ......

NOTES.—1. Special attention is drawn to the instructions printed on the second page.
2. Unit will fill in all particulars in block letters.
3. Part III must be given up to the Railway Company at the British Port of Disembarkation before commencing the forward rail journey.

*[actual dimensions 95mm x 120mm]*

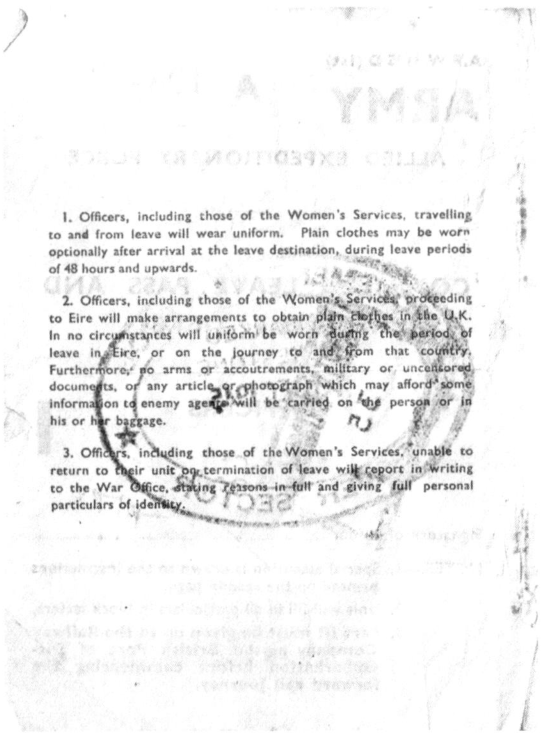
1. Officers, including those of the Women's Services, travelling to and from leave will wear uniform. Plain clothes may be worn optionally after arrival at the leave destination, during leave periods of 48 hours and upwards.

2. Officers, including those of the Women's Services, proceeding to Eire will make arrangements to obtain plain clothes in the U.K. In no circumstances will uniform be worn during the period of leave in Eire, or on the journey to and from that country. Furthermore, no arms or accoutrements, military or uncensored documents, or any article or photograph which may afford some information to enemy agents will be carried on the person or in his or her baggage.

3. Officers, including those of the Women's Services, unable to return to their unit on termination of leave will report in writing to the War Office, stating reasons in full and giving full personal particulars of identity.

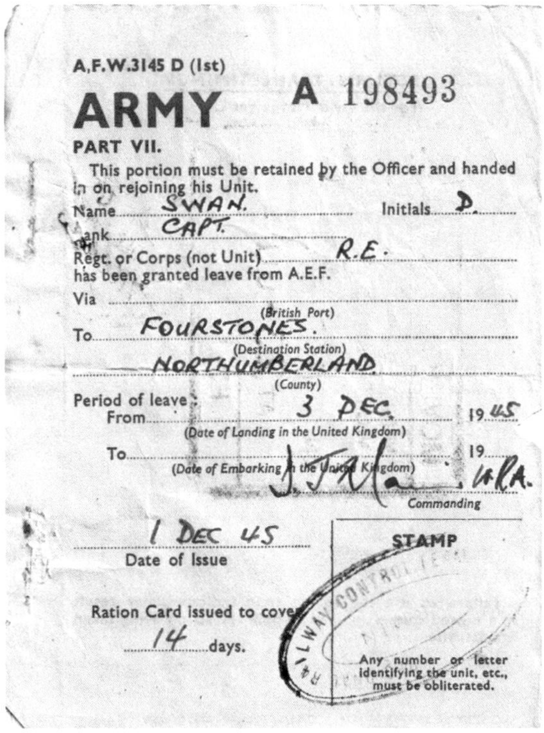
A.F.W.3145 D (Ist)

ARMY A 198493

PART VII.

This portion must be retained by the Officer and handed in on rejoining his Unit.

Name ...SWAN... Initials ...D...
Rank ...CAPT...
Regt. or Corps (not Unit) ...R.E...
has been granted leave from A.E.F.
Via ......
(British Port)
To ...FOURSTONES...
(Destination Station)
...NORTHUMBERLAND...
(County)
Period of leave: From ...3 DEC... 19 45
(Date of Landing in the United Kingdom)
To ...... 19...
(Date of Embarking in the United Kingdom)
...... Commanding

1 DEC 45
Date of Issue

Ration Card issued to cover ...14... days.

STAMP

Any number or letter identifying the unit, etc., must be obliterated.

The first instruction on this page (left) states: "Officers, including those of the Women's Services, travelling to and from leave will wear uniform. Plain clothes may be worn optionally after arrival at the leave destination, during leave periods of 48 hours and upwards". The second instruction goes on to prohibit the wearing of uniform while travelling to, from, and while in Eire and also prohibits carrying any document, or other articles, or photographs which may afford some information to enemy agents during that period. Despite Eire being neutral, some members of the Irish Army felt that they should be involved in the fight against Hitler and what he stood for and resigned from the Irish Army to join the British Armed Forces. For this they were officially listed as Deserters and it was not until May 2013 that they were officially pardoned.

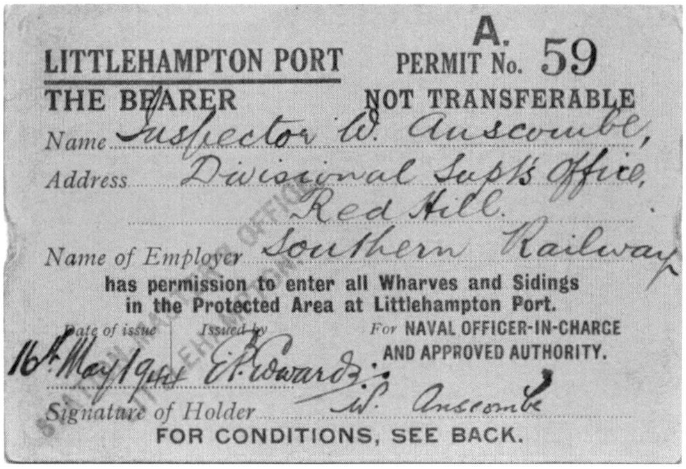

A.
LITTLEHAMPTON PORT PERMIT No. 59
THE BEARER NOT TRANSFERABLE
Name Inspector W. Anscombe,
Address Divisional Supts Office,
Red Hill.
Name of Employer Southern Railway
has permission to enter all Wharves and Sidings in the Protected Area at Littlehampton Port.
Date of issue 16th May 19[illegible] | Issued by E. Edwards | For NAVAL OFFICER-IN-CHARGE AND APPROVED AUTHORITY.
Signature of Holder W. Anscombe
FOR CONDITIONS, SEE BACK.

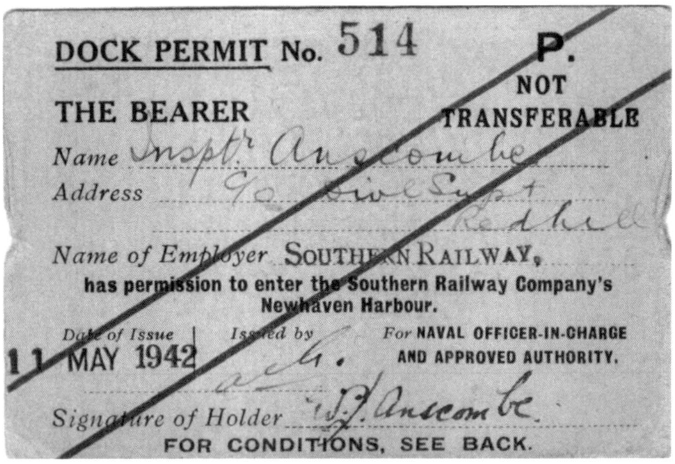

DOCK PERMIT No. 514 P.
THE BEARER NOT TRANSFERABLE
Name Inspr Anscombe
Address c/o Divl Supt
Redhill
Name of Employer SOUTHERN RAILWAY,
has permission to enter the Southern Railway Company's Newhaven Harbour.
Date of Issue 11 MAY 1942 | Issued by | For NAVAL OFFICER-IN-CHARGE AND APPROVED AUTHORITY.
Signature of Holder W.J. Anscombe.
FOR CONDITIONS, SEE BACK.

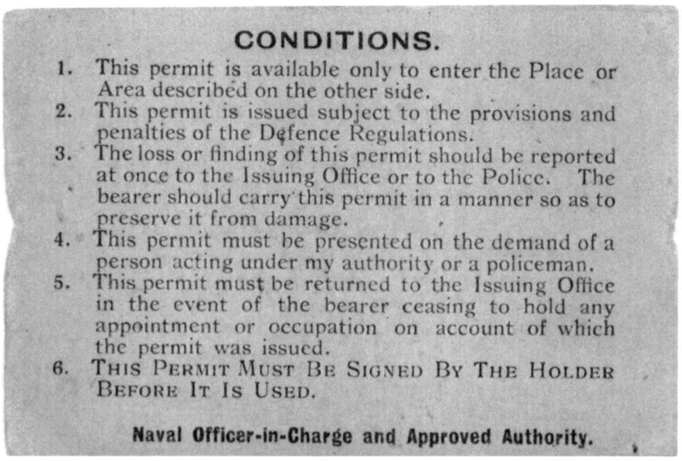

CONDITIONS.

1. This permit is available only to enter the Place or Area described on the other side.
2. This permit is issued subject to the provisions and penalties of the Defence Regulations.
3. The loss or finding of this permit should be reported at once to the Issuing Office or to the Police. The bearer should carry this permit in a manner so as to preserve it from damage.
4. This permit must be presented on the demand of a person acting under my authority or a policeman.
5. This permit must be returned to the Issuing Office in the event of the bearer ceasing to hold any appointment or occupation on account of which the permit was issued.
6. THIS PERMIT MUST BE SIGNED BY THE HOLDER BEFORE IT IS USED.

Naval Officer-in-Charge and Approved Authority.

As can be seen from the previous leave passes, South Coast ports were vital links with Europe and passes were necessary, even for Southern Railway employees, to enter the protected areas of these ports. Newhaven continues as a ferry port and the current operators, LD Lines/Transmanche Ferries have plans for improvements which include a modern terminal. Commercial activity is now a shadow of its former volume at Littlehampton where it is confined to the import of aggregate for local asphalt production being handled at the one remaining commercial wharf.

A selection of leave tickets. The railways were not the only means of transport for short term leave as the two part Compton Basset ticket demonstrates. The R.A.F. station closed in the 1960's. Royal Naval Air Service Machrihanish is a former Royal Navy Air Service station that now incorporates Campbeltown Airport. It was sold in 2012 for £1 to a consortium who hope to develop the site for the benefit of the local community.

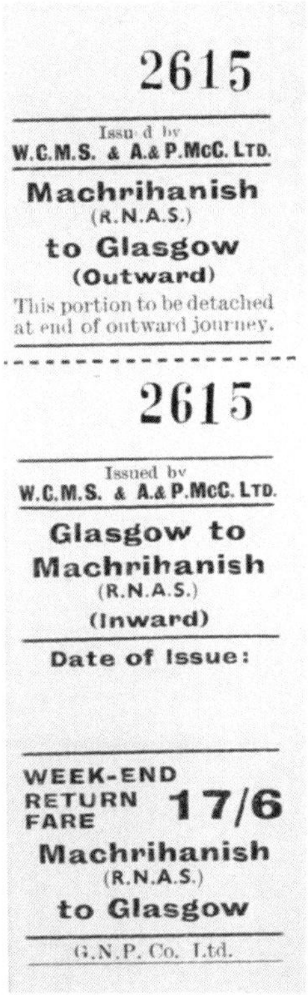


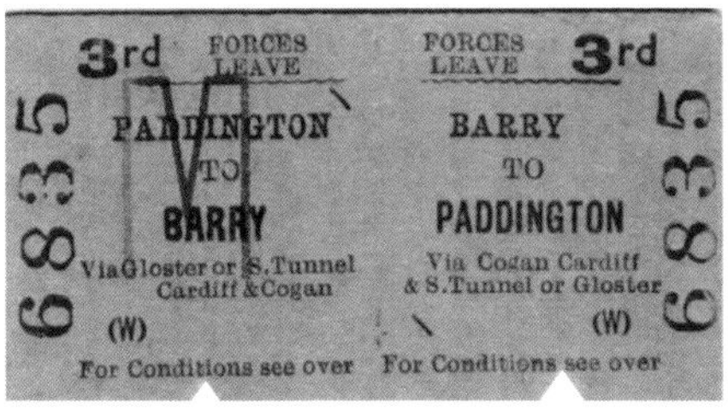


A selection of military duty tickets. The Midland Railway opened a station named Henlow some distance from the village of the same name, as part of its new line from Bedford to Hitchin. Passenger traffic over the Bedford to Hitchin section was minimal and services were reduced to a shuttle by 1880. The establishment of R.A.F. Henlow at the end of the First World War increased passenger and freight traffic. The activity continued after the war when the base became the location of the R.A.F. Signals Engineering Establishment, and a depot for the repair and construction of aircraft as well as a training centre for the engineers. It became the School of Aeronautical Engineering in 1924. To reflect this development, the railway station's name was changed in 1933 to Henlow Camp. The line closed in 1962.

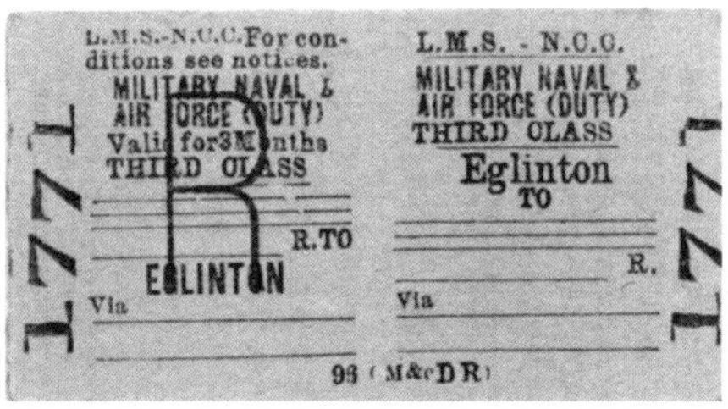


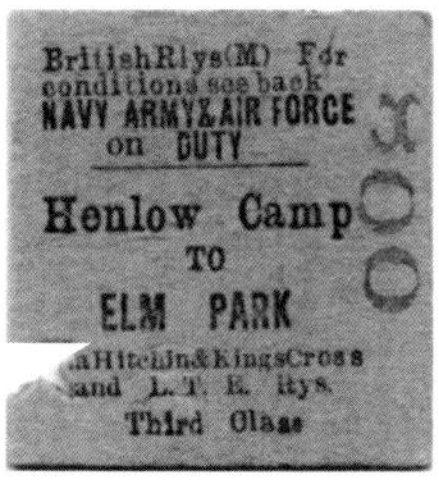


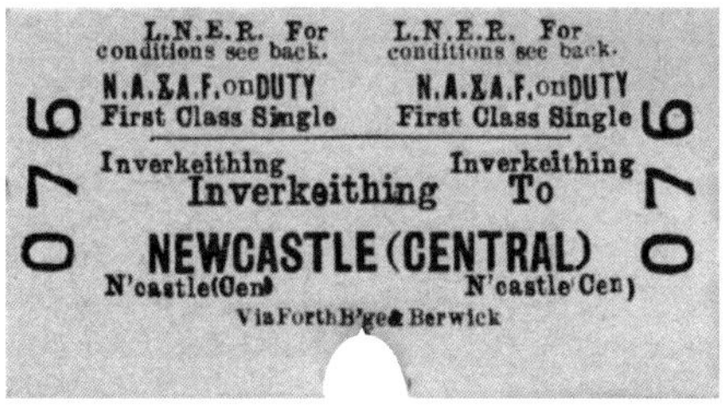


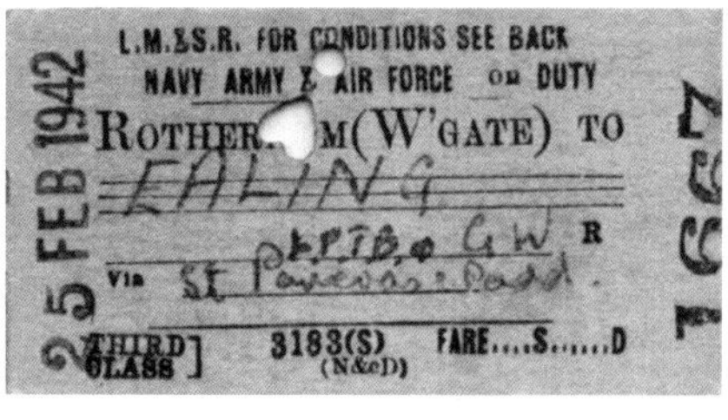

A large number of workers was necessary at home to provide support to the fighting forces. The Ardeer peninsula was the site of the British Dynamite Factory built by Alfred Bernhard Nobel in 1871, who went on to create what was described then as the largest explosives factory in the world. At its peak, the site employed almost 13,000 workers in a fairly remote location. and had its own railway station by July 1926 which closed in 1966 Nobel was a founding member of Imperial Chemical Industries. In January 2008 ICI was taken over by Akzo Nobel.

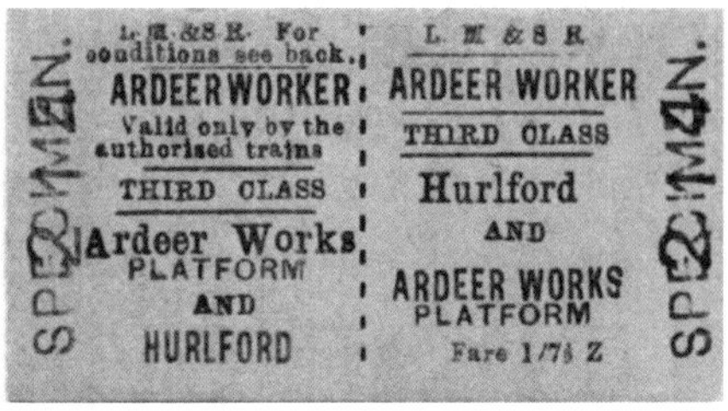
L.M.&S.R. For conditions see back.
ARDEERWORKER
Valid only by the authorised trains
THIRD CLASS
Ardeer Works PLATFORM
AND
HURLFORD

L.M.&S.R.
ARDEER WORKER
THIRD CLASS
Hurlford
AND
ARDEER WORKS PLATFORM
Fare 1/7½ Z

Rosyth Dockyard construction work began in 1909. Designed to provide fleet maintenance facilities in the event of war with Germany, it was eventually completed in 1916. The First World War saw the dockyard mainly engaged in repair and refit work. However, post-war economies saw the temporary closure of Rosyth. The declaration of war in 1939 saw the immediate re-establishment of Rosyth. After the war, the need to modernize the dockyards eventually led to the creation of multi-million pound nuclear refit centres at Devonport, Chatham and Rosyth. Changes to the yards continued into the next decade with a further round of cut-backs. Rosyth is no longer a direct part of the Admiralty administrative structure, their privatised status means they must compete against each other. While this presentation was being written a further round of cuts affecting, amongst others, Rosyth was announced. Of which more later.

LONDON & NORTH EASTERN RAILWAY
No. 0128 ADMIRALTY WORKMAN'S TICKET
THIRD CLASS
AVAILABLE BETWEEN
DYSART or SINCLAIRTOWN
AND
INVERKEITHING, ROSYTH HALT or ROSYTH DOCKYARD
Name of Holder M F
Signature of Holder
Dockyard Ticket No.
FOR CONDITIONS SEE BACK

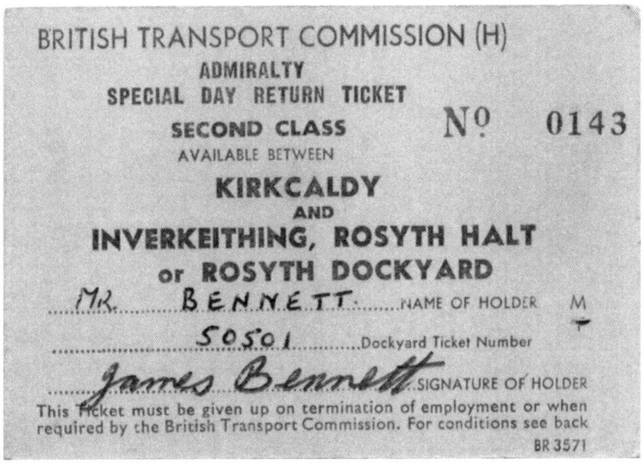
BRITISH TRANSPORT COMMISSION (H)
ADMIRALTY
SPECIAL DAY RETURN TICKET
SECOND CLASS Nº 0143
AVAILABLE BETWEEN
KIRKCALDY
AND
INVERKEITHING, ROSYTH HALT
or ROSYTH DOCKYARD
MR BENNETT NAME OF HOLDER M F
50501 Dockyard Ticket Number
James Bennett SIGNATURE OF HOLDER
This Ticket must be given up on termination of employment or when required by the British Transport Commission. For conditions see back
BR 3571

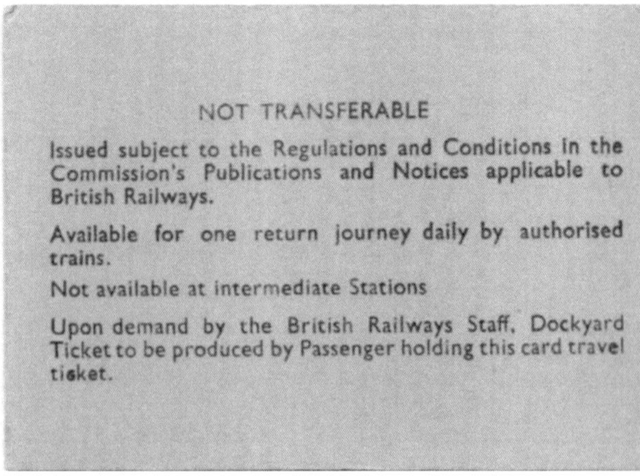
NOT TRANSFERABLE
Issued subject to the Regulations and Conditions in the Commission's Publications and Notices applicable to British Railways.
Available for one return journey daily by authorised trains.
Not available at intermediate Stations
Upon demand by the British Railways Staff, Dockyard Ticket to be produced by Passenger holding this card travel ticket.

Royal Ordnance Factory – 38 was located adjacent to the East Coast Main Line railway at Ranskill, Nottinghamshire. Its construction was approved in 1940 and it was built as an almost self-contained, explosive factory producing Cordite. It was the last Cordite-producing Royal Ordnance Factory to be built in the UK in World War II and was the smallest of the three Cordite Royal Ordnance Factories. It was connected to the railway line, with its own private sidings. It employed, at maximum production, some 4,000 people. It ceased production in 1945, at the end of World War II, but was retained by the Royal Ordnance Factory organisation until 1975 on a care and maintenance basis.

Conscription into the armed forces of agricultural workers led to shortages of workers on farms and forests. The Women's Timber Corps was formed in 1942, three years after the formation of the Women's Land Army. An assortment of Farming and Forestry Camp tickets and Workers on the Land.

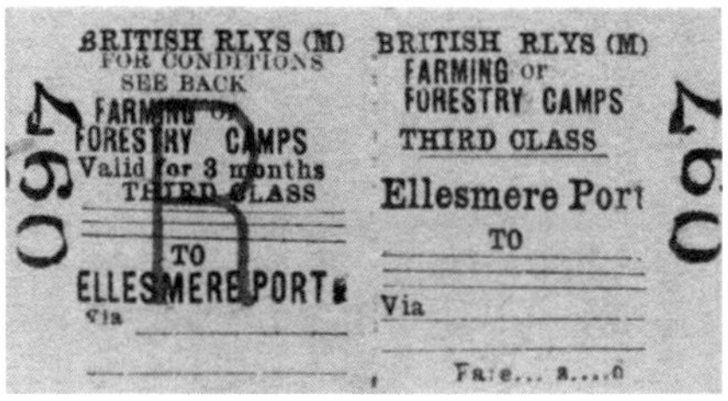


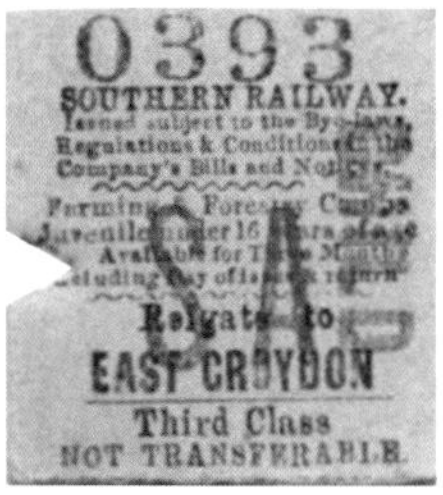


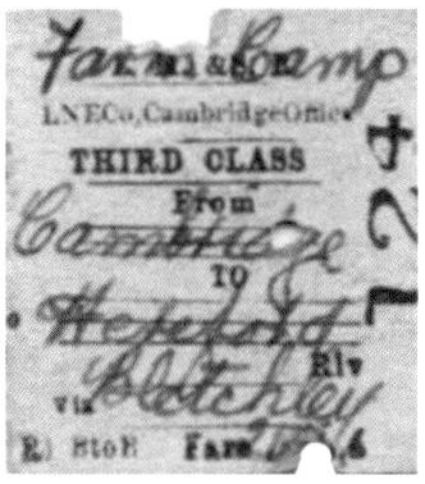


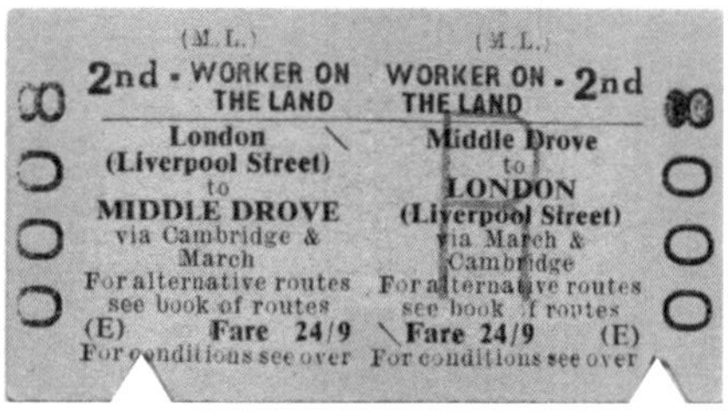


The Merchant Navy had an important role in keeping Britain fed but, despite Royal Naval support, convoys suffered heavy losses. The two Southern Railway tickets are dated during the war while the British Rail ones date from the 1950/60s. As with the armed forces, demarcation between officers and men existed in the Merchant Navy. Seamen travelled 3rd class, officers 1st class.

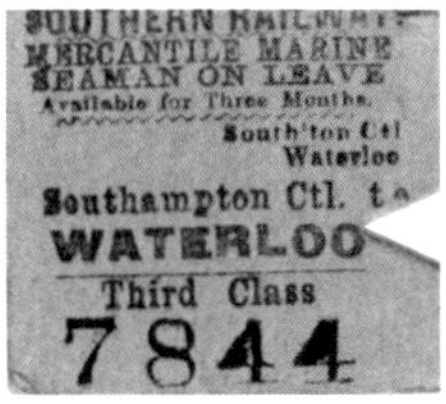

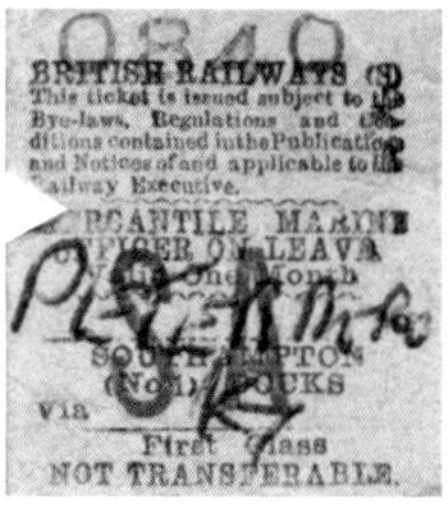


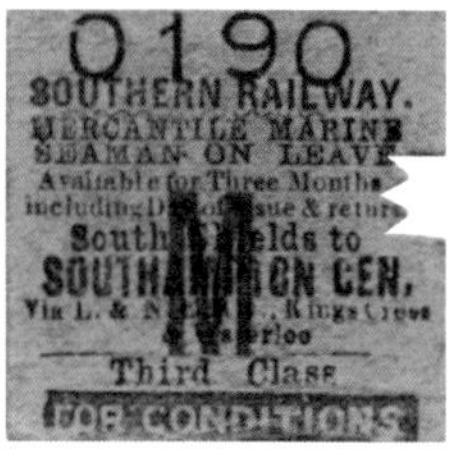

The unpretentious ticket from Stranraer belies a wealth of history attached to Stranraer's birth, expansion and finally demise as a port. Stranraer was first mentioned in the 14th century although there may have been a settlement there from as early as Roman times when a Roman road ran from Gatehouse of Fleet, via Dunragit, to Stranraer and continued up towards Cairnryan. Stranraer's life as a town really began in 1595 when King James VI gave Stranraer trading rights and a market. In the 17th and 18th centuries the town quickly expanded due to trade in textiles, tanning and fishing. Stranraer, has its history centred around the port with the first harbour known to be in existence in the mid 18th century. By the 1830's steam packets were making regular trips to Glasgow, Girvan and Belfast.

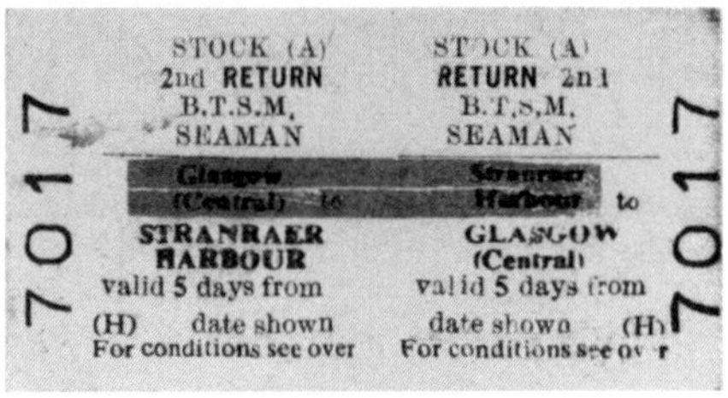
STOCK (A)
2nd RETURN
B.T.S.M.
SEAMAN
STRANRAER HARBOUR
valid 5 days from
(H) date shown
For conditions see over
RETURN 2nd
GLASGOW (Central)
7017

Next the railway came to Stranraer in 1861, which, in those days came direct from Dumfries. The following year, the railway was extended to meet right up with the harbour and link up Portpatrick too. It was in 1862 when the official ferry service to Belfast began. Stranraer and nearby Kirkcolm played an important role in the second World War, with Winston Churchill taking a trip in a Boeing flying boat from Stranraer to the USA in 1942. Also during the War, Cairnryan became No. 2 Military Port, and three harbour piers and a military railway linking the village with nearby Stranraer were built by the army. Thousands of troops were based locally in military camps. At the end of the War the Atlantic U Boat fleet surrendered in Loch Ryan and was anchored there before being towed to sea and sunk.

P. P. & W. Joint Rys.
645
KIRKCOWAN TO
GLASGOW(ST.ENOCH)(GSW
VIA DUMFRIES
Third] 16(S) [Class
GLASGOW(ST. E. GSW)
TURN OVER)

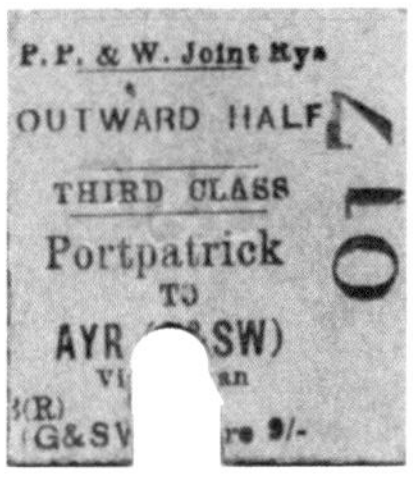
P. P. & W. Joint Rys
OUTWARD HALF
THIRD CLASS
Portpatrick
TO
017

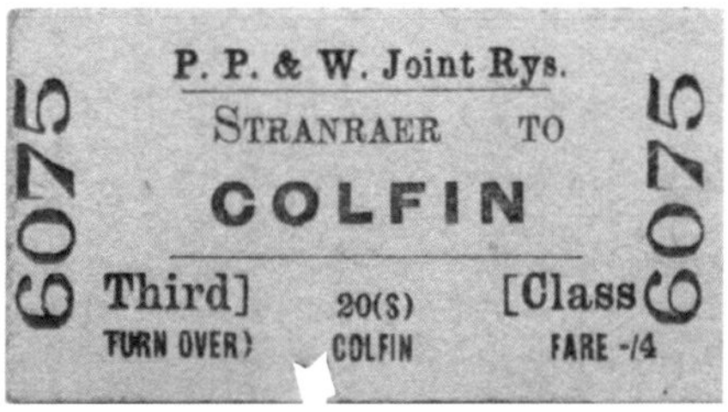
P. P. & W. Joint Rys.
STRANRAER TO
COLFIN
Third] 20(S) [Class
TURN OVER) COLFIN FARE -/4
6075

The town lost its direct rail connection to Dumfries in 1965. The seaman holding ticket 7017, that we met earlier, would have further to go to find a boat these days as in 2011 the town ceased to be a ferry port when Stena Line moved their ferry services closer to the mouth of Loch Ryan, near Old House Point Cairnryan, a few miles north of Stranraer and close to open waters as P&O Ferries had done at an earlier date.

Stranraer - Belfast
Stena Line
BOARDING CARD
IMPORTANT SAFETY INSTRUCTIONS
1. You are required to pay attention to safety announcements on board and to familiarise yourself with the contents of Emergency Notices which are posted at Muster stations (see Muster Station sign below), in the main passenger areas.
2. Non-landing passengers must report to the Purser's Office on arrival in port of destination.
3. Baggage must not block access to safety equipment or passenger escapes.
1. Vous êtes priés de faire attention aux annonces de sécurité faites à bord et de vous familiariser avec la signalisation d' urgence qui est affichée aux points de rassemblement suités dans les principaux locaux passagers.
2. Tous les passagers qui ne débaquent pas doivent se rendre au bureau d' information dès l'arrivée du navire au Port de destination.
3. Les bagages ne doivent pas géner les accès à l'équipement de sécurité ni les issues de secours
YOU MUST RETAIN
THIS SECTION
TO PURCHASE
DUTY FREE
0020403

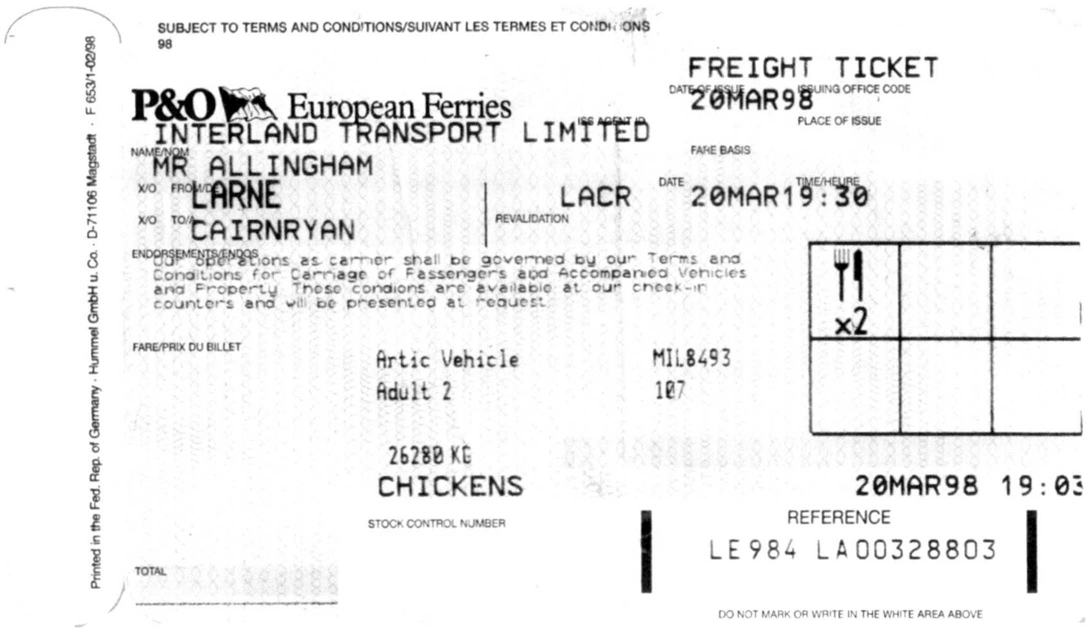


A final look at the home front with Bomb Damage Worker by special train from the South Coast and Civil Defence and Home Guard from London stations.

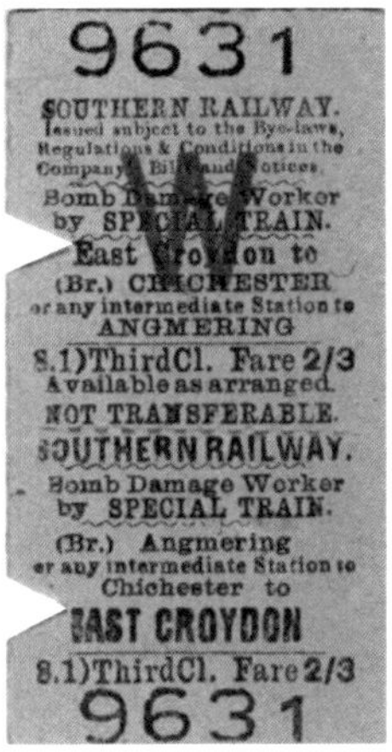


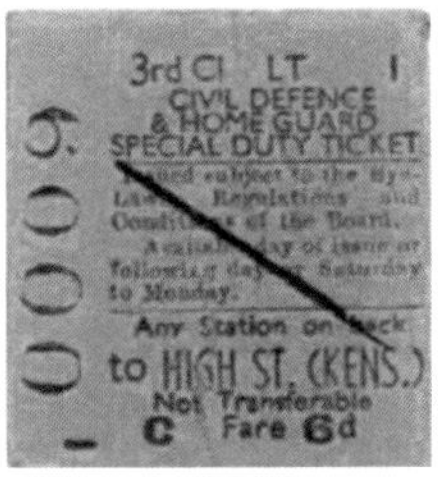


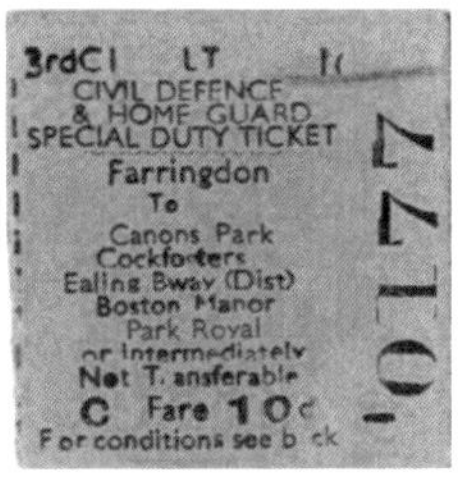


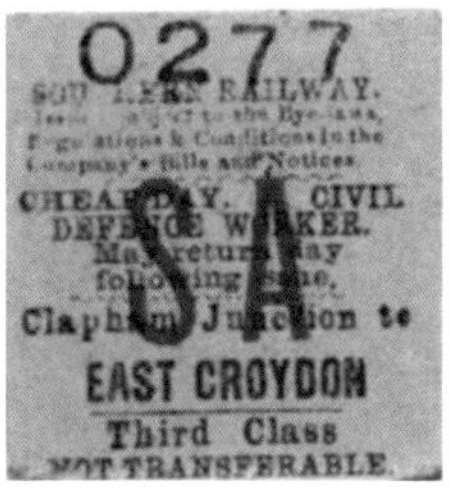


My family moved to Bristol after the war where there had been an extensive tramway system, but this had been damaged to such an extent in the war that it was beyond repair. Three pre-war workmen's tickets dating from 1918 and about 1933.

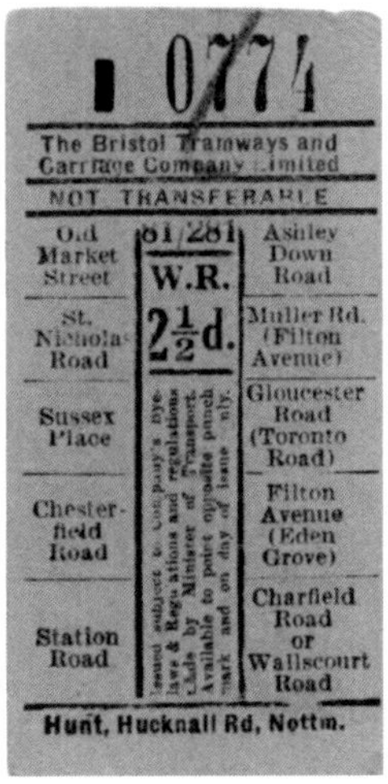


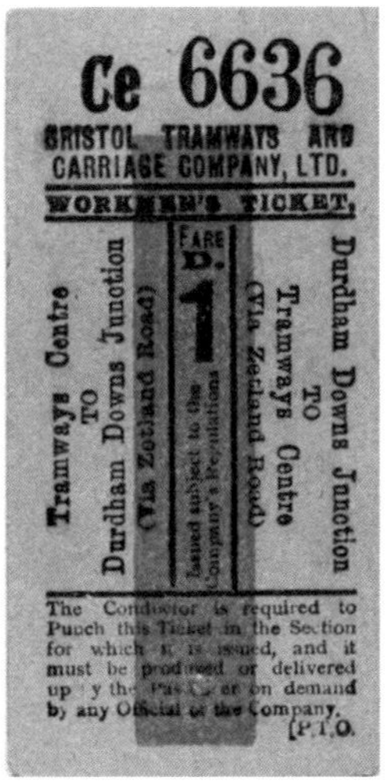


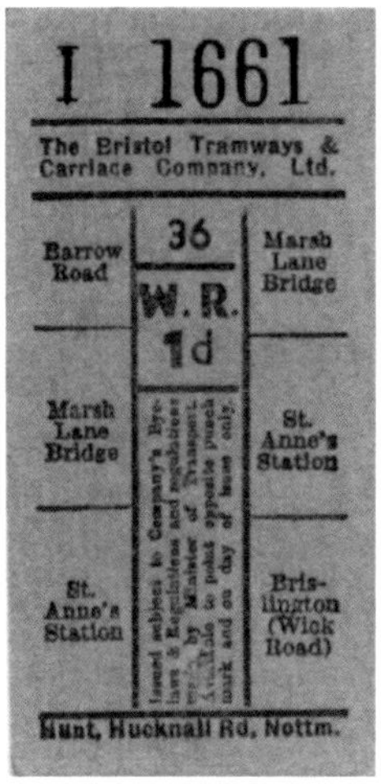

With the closure of the tramway, geographical Workmen's tickets on the buses were replaced by a new set of numerical stage punch tickets. These tickets were longer than normal due to the blank space at the top and bottom of the ticket.

In 1942 Workmen's returns followed the Single fare new design. I just scraped in to see the use of Punch tickets. The end of workmen's returns came on 14th March 1955. There had been minor changes after 1942 and three are illustrated here. The date of issue code is the letter prefix of the ticket number on the 5½d, while on the other two it is the letter at the top of the centre column.

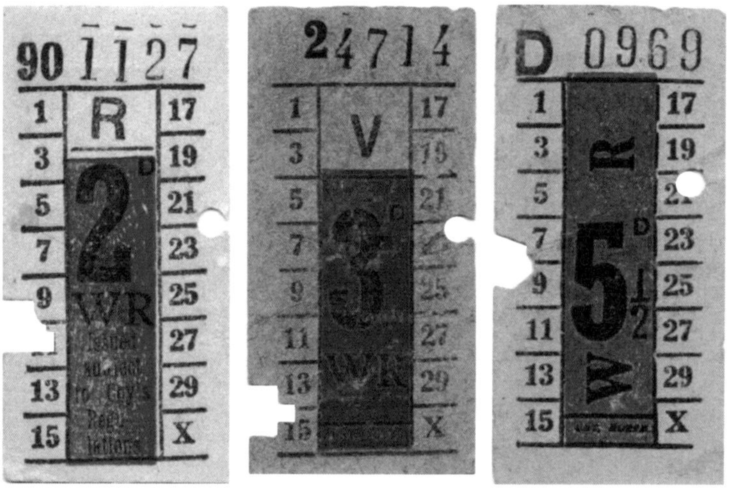


A couple of Bristol's later season tickets. The City B Line season pre dates the Plus Bus concept. It could only be used on services 8 and 9 between Temple Meads station and Queens Road and was only valid in conjunction with a rail season ticket.

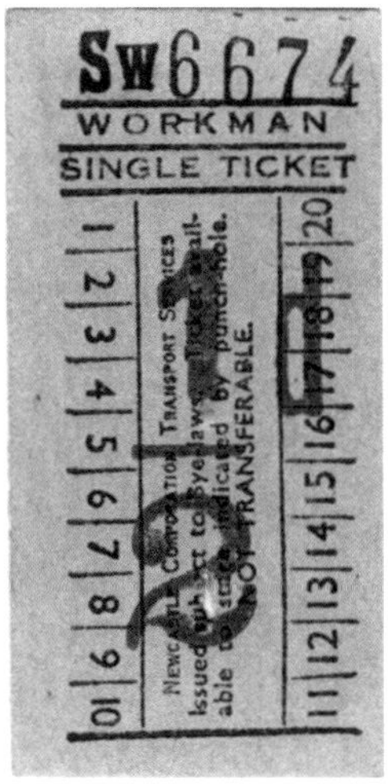


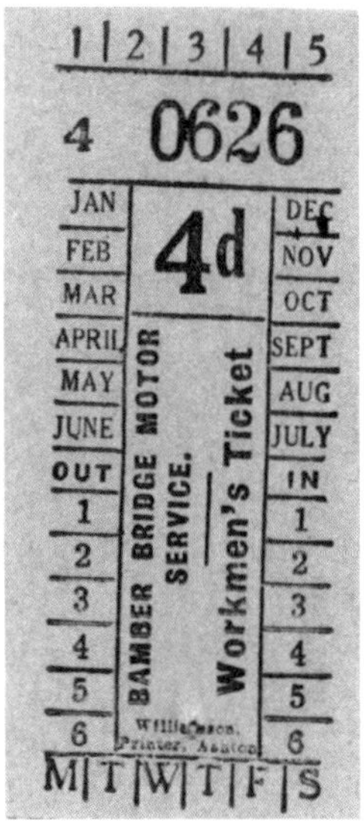


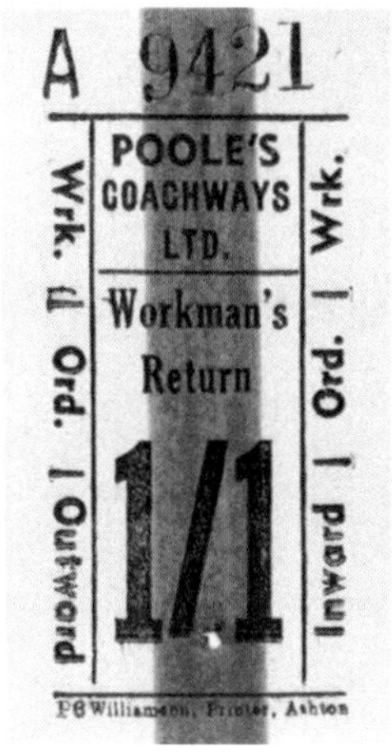


Earlier I was surprised at a return ticket for 2d, how about a Workman's Single at a half Penny? (£0.002083), or was it an auxiliary ticket to save printing a range of ½d tickets?

A Bamber Bridge Workmen's 4d return. This ticket was valid for a second journey within 8 days of the date of issue.

The Poole's Workman's Return has an identity crisis as there is provision for an ordinary return in the side punch spaces

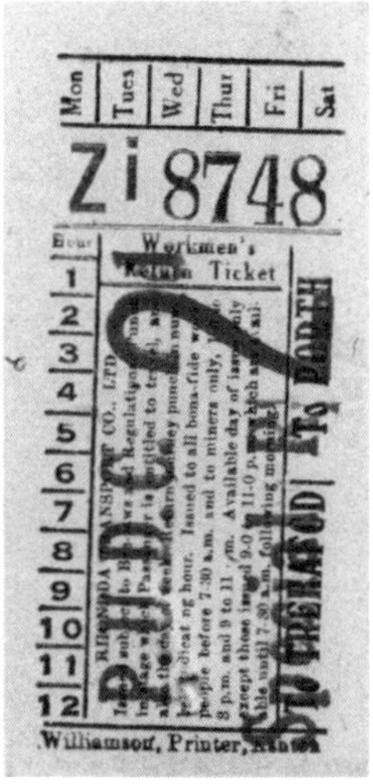


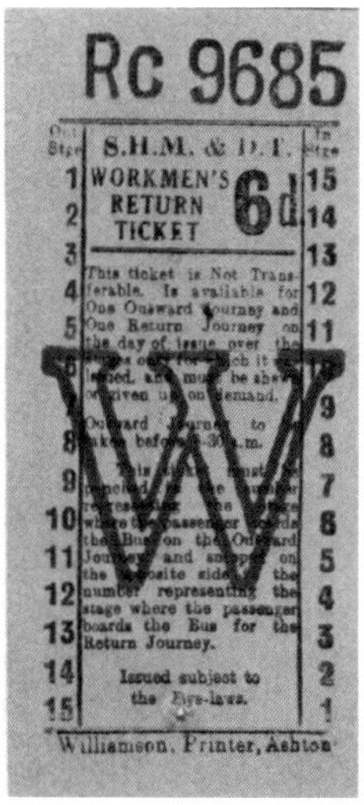


This Rhondda Transport Co Ltd has lengthy time restrictions including being only issued to bona fide workers before 7.30am but also to miners between 1.00pm and 8.00pm and 9.00pm to 11.00pm for return the same day, except for miners' tickets issued between 9.00pm to 11.00pm which were valid to 7.30am the following morning. The complex time provisions are to fit round the miners' various shifts.

Whilst S.H.M. & D.T. (Stalybridge, Hyde, Mossley & Dukinfield Transport Board) has a simpler qualifying time of just 8.30am for the outward journey.

Weekly tickets can be confusing as a week varies between five and seven days. The Advance Bus service and the Pontypridd Council Transport believe that it is seven days.

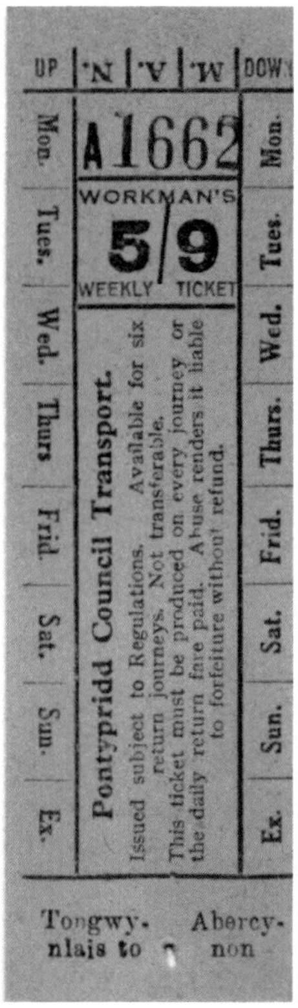


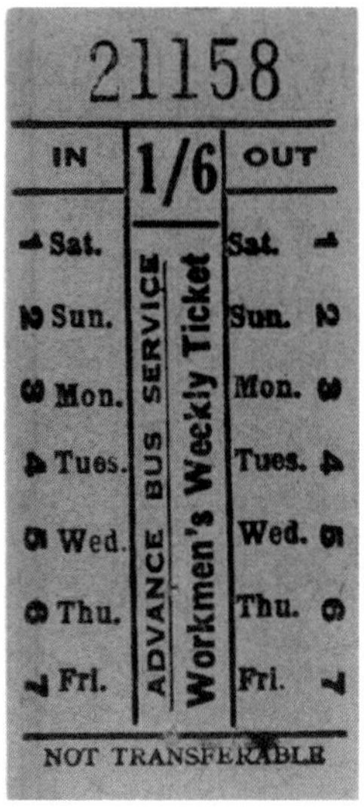


Cumberland Motor Services play safe and call their tickets Worker's Ten Journey tickets – five consecutive days Monday to Friday or 12 Journey tickets valid for one return journey for six consecutive days, excluding Sunday unless bought after 6.00pm on Sunday.

Walter Alexander are less trusting of their passengers as their 24 Journey Weekly ticket - two return journeys each day Monday to Saturday - has to be signed in ink three lines up from the bottom. The two return journeys were to allow workers the opportunity to return home for lunch.

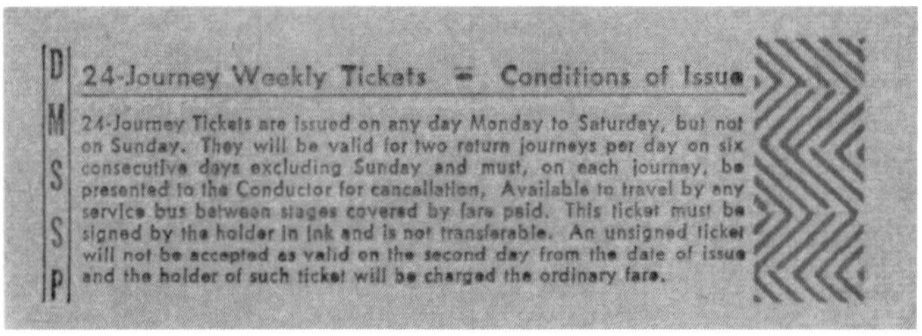

Workers' seasons, and in general all road seasons, have had growing security measures such as laminated cards and the requirement of an accompanying photocard. Photocards are probably thought of as modern requirement but they have been around for a long time. The one on the left was a Commercial Travellers' Great Northern Railway Certificate of Identity impressed with the year 1899 in gold on the back cover. On the right are the vouchers for use with a G.W.R. certificate of which more later.

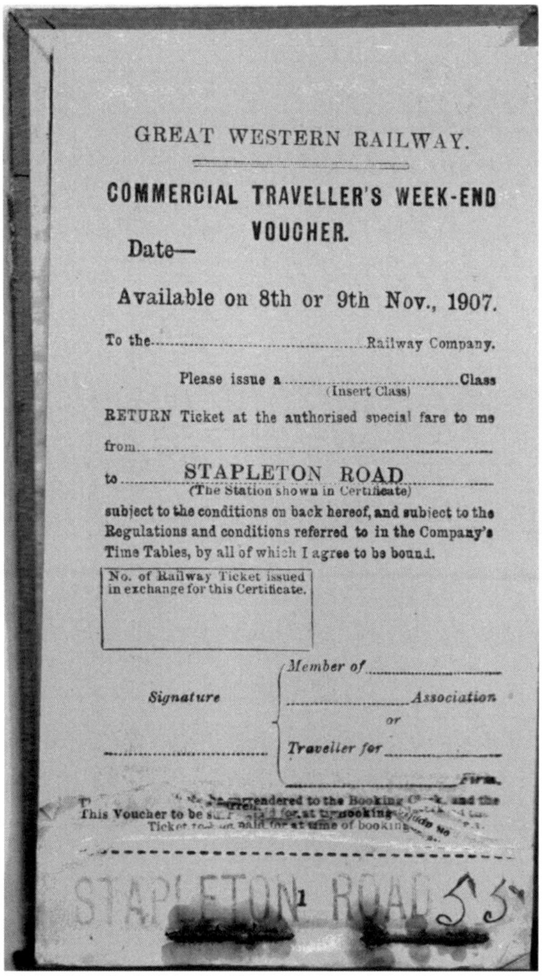


Not all firms and businesses were large enough to warrant their own run of tickets. Over the years attitudes have changed towards workmen with "trains for the working classes" progressing to "by authorised trains", to just reference to workmen, and finally "Early Morning Return" available to all within the time limits. Some of the tickets are issued in packs of 5 or 6 available only on the day specified on the front of the ticket during the week commencing on the date on the back or as coupons torn from a sheet. Some tickets not only state the day of validity but also specify the train.

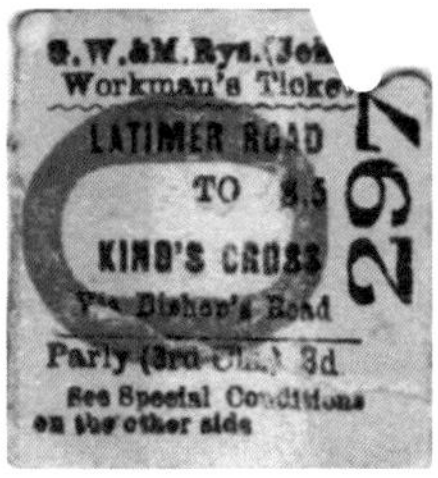


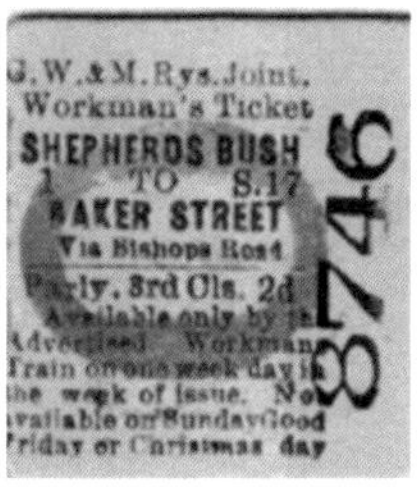


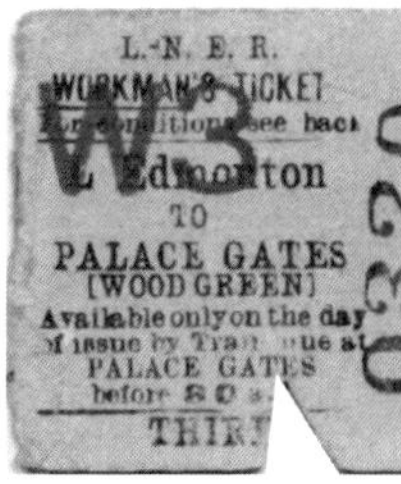


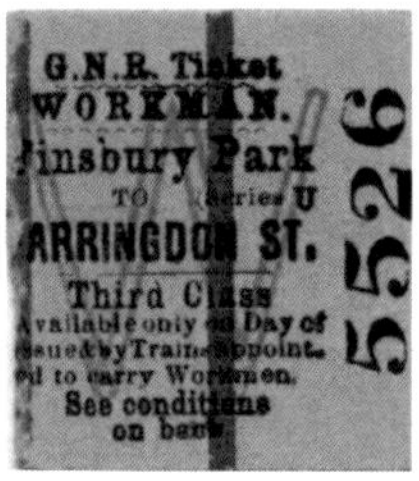

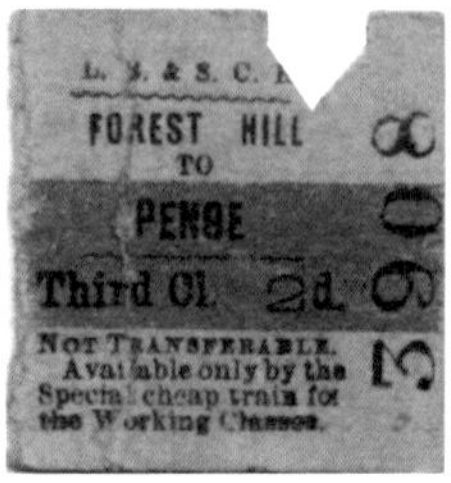

There seem to be workmen's tickets to suit all requirements ranging from Early Morning to Middle or Afternoon; Late; and finally Night, servicing the shift pattern of the particular industry and location involved.

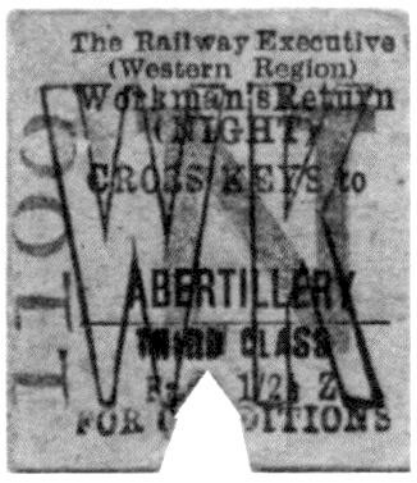


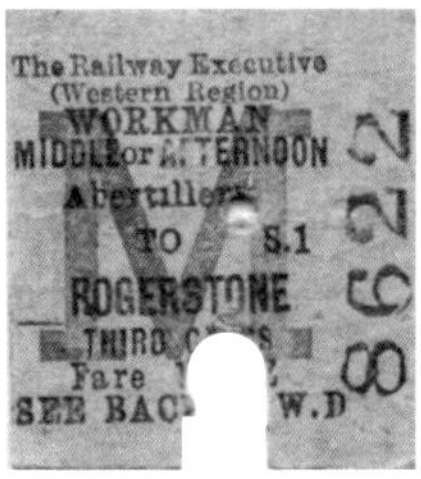


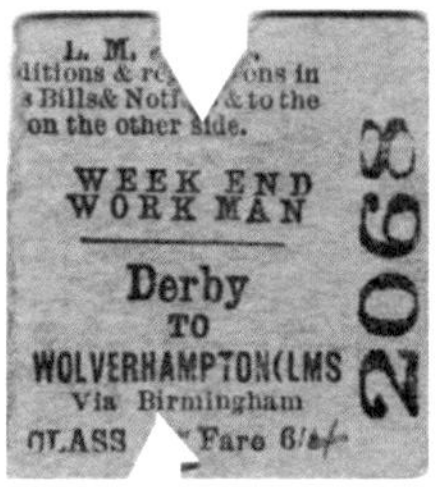


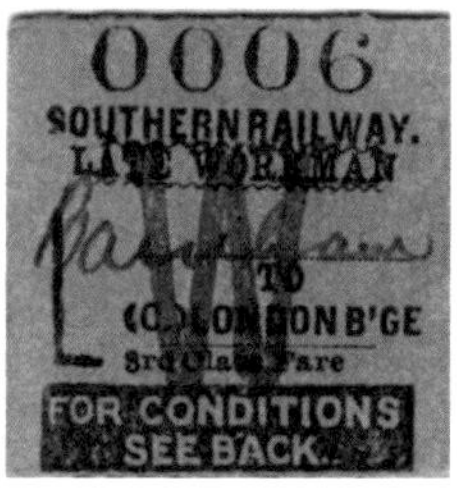


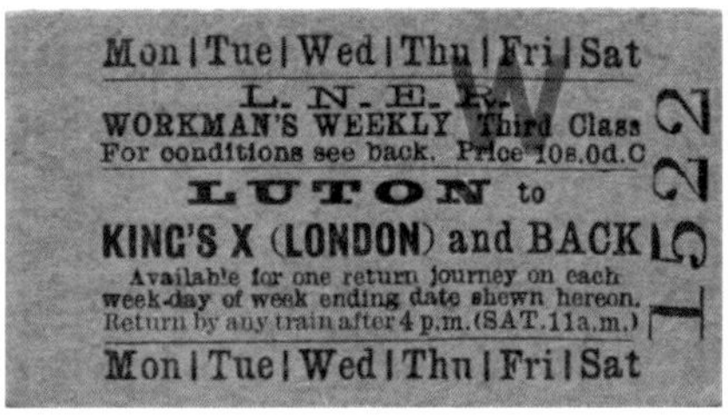


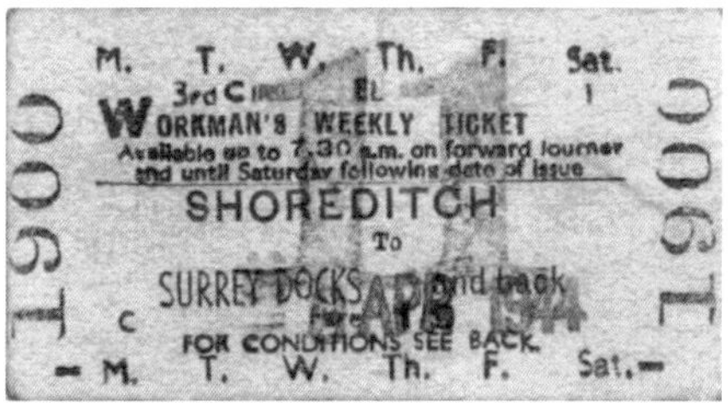


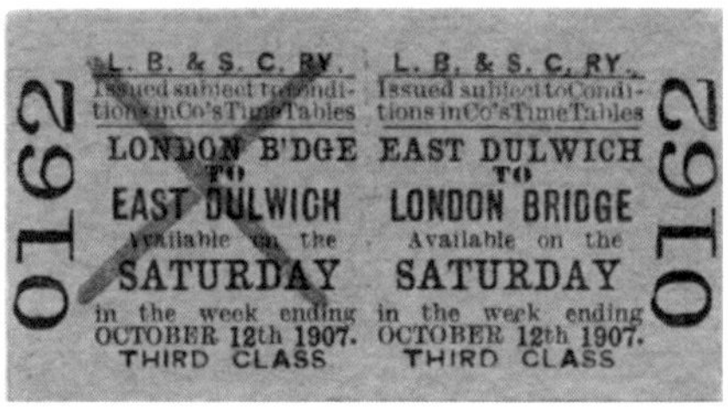


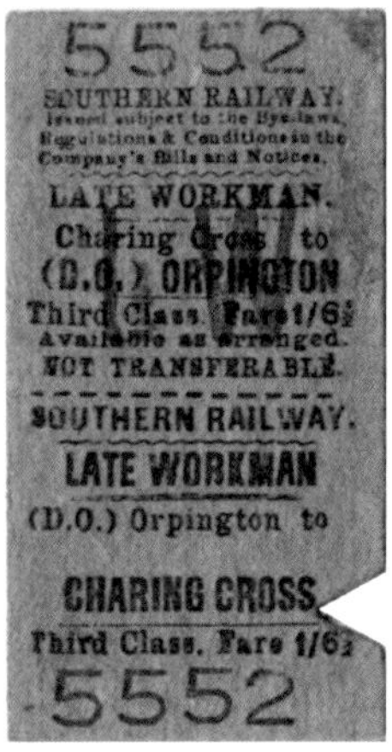


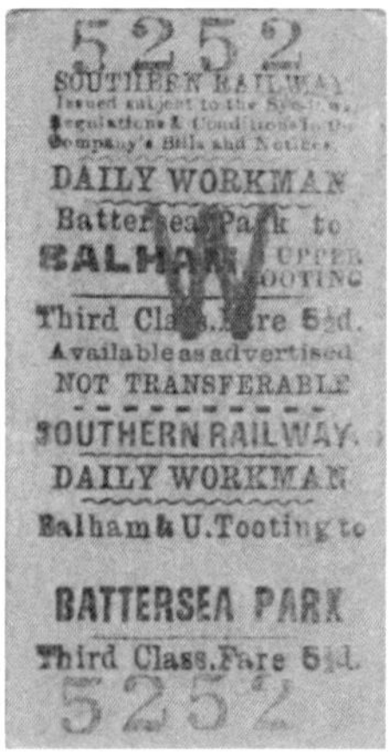


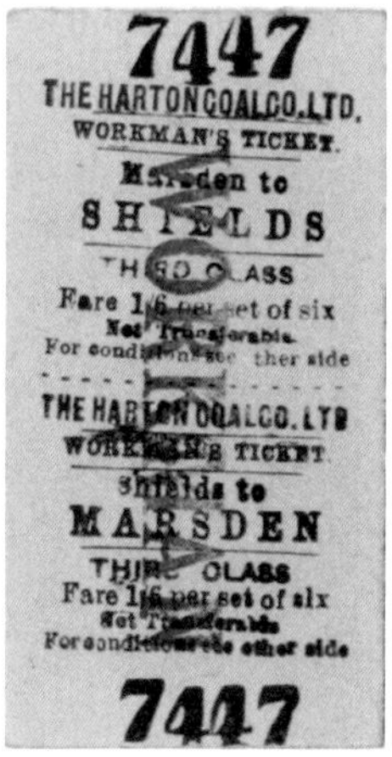

Not all the tickets are bought and paid for on the bus and the Prestwell's appear to come in a packs of 12 Journeys, a ticket with an overprinted W for the outward leg and a plain ticket for the return, for which the cover is illustrated. Also illustrated is a Newcastle Corporation Transport also with 12 journeys at a cost of 3/6 without instructions for use. Finally a Reading Corporation Transport 2d Workman Ticket, the bottom half of which is kept by the conductor and the top half handed back.

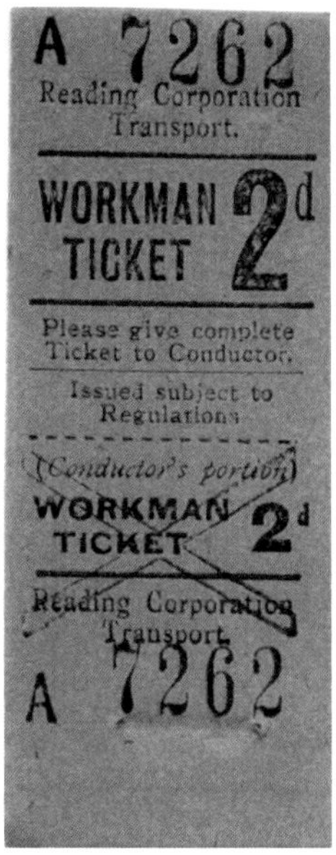

This also applied to Railway tickets. Maritime Stores Limited is a voucher for the employees to receive a second class ordinary return ticket from Liverpool to Birkenhead.

Alfred Holt was a Victorian, engineer, merchant and shipowner. Originally trading as The Blue Funnel Line, which came to an end in 1988. The Railway Exec./L.M.R. voucher is dated 13MY49 on the back. This and the next few illustrations are rather depressing as they are part of the history of once great industries who are now defunct or not as great as they once were.

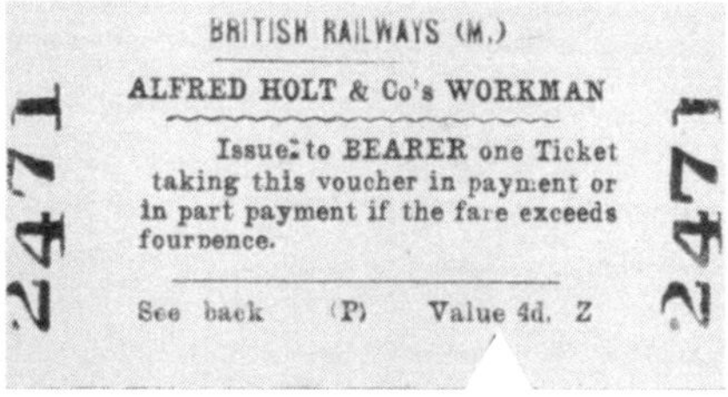


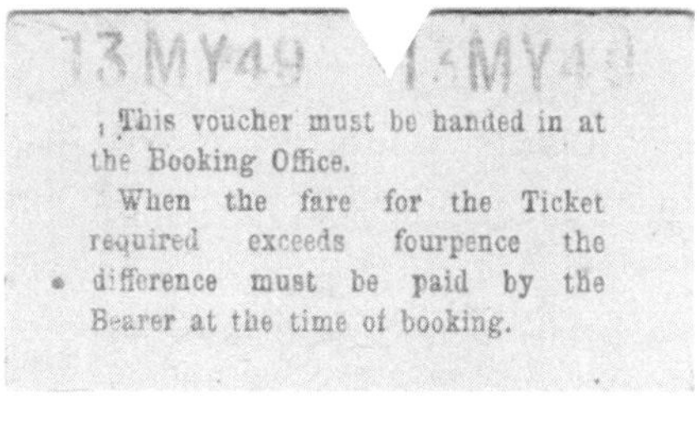


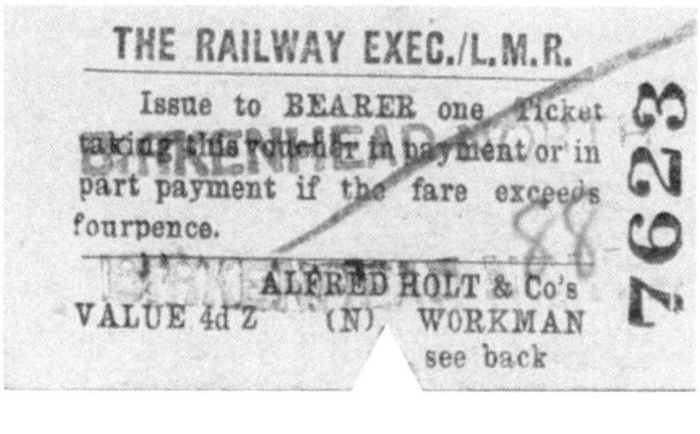

The British Aerospace site at Brough dates back to 1916 when the Blackburn Aeroplane & Motor Company built a new factory there. From mergers and re-namings the company became British Aerospace plc by September 2011 when the company announced that manufacturing at the site was to end in the middle of 2013. How fortunes can change for the workforce in a relatively short space of time. In Ken Pudsey's 2007 Presidential address he was able to say that".... *at Brough there is a very busy aircraft factory."* Four years later Brough was faced with the loss of all manufacturing work on the site. Following lobbying and protest some jobs were saved, but at a heavy price as there was a large number of redundancies over a period of twenty-one months. BAE Systems came under threat again recently with a 1,775 proposed cut in the shipbuilding workforce. Some see this as political interference, which the government hotly denies.

IBM Halt opened on 9th May 1978 to serve what was at that time a thriving computer manufacturing plant employing over 4,000 people. Part of the site was sold off to other companies, some of which have since closed. By June 2009 half of the buildings had been demolished and the site has been rebranded as Valley Park.

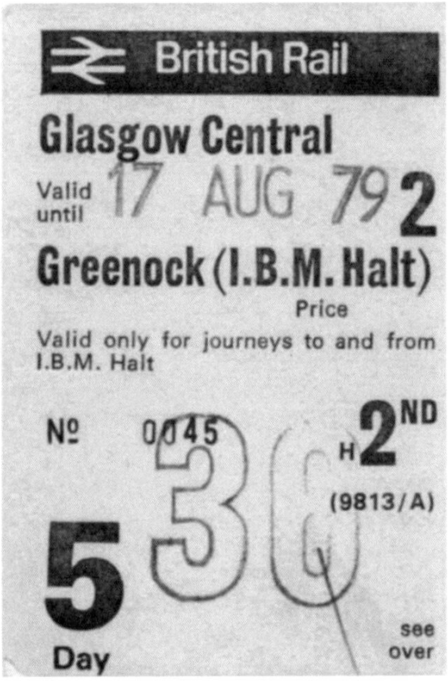

Cement Mills Halt on the Isle of Wight, was opened by 1909 to serve the workers at the nearby West Medina mills which produced Portland and Medina cement. This included the contract to supply all the Portland cement used in the construction of the fourth Eddystone lighthouse. The trackbed now forms part of the Newport to Cowes cycleway.

In 1980, Barclays Bank International, with offices in Poole, expanded its business to include commercial credit and took over American Credit Corporation, renaming it Barclays American Corporation. Tracing what became of a particular name is not made easier by large groups re-organising and renaming themselves at frequent intervals. Although Barclays Bank plc has its head office in Canary Wharf there still seems to be an administrative presence in Poole which provides support functions for Global Retail and Commercial Banking operations. This is much like the company I worked for which split the "Front Office" in the City of London from the "Back Office" in Norwich and Witham.

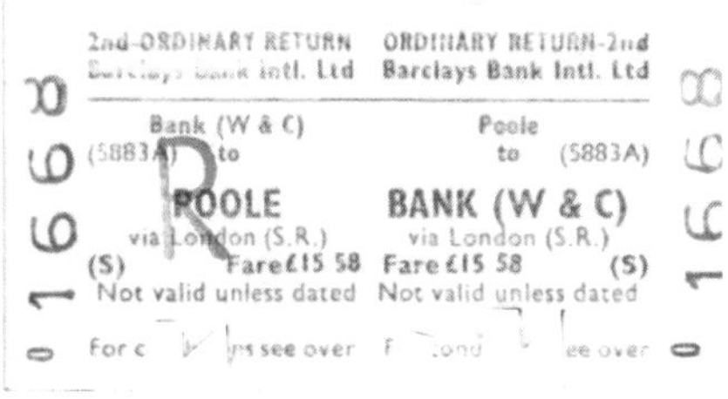


Josiah Wedgwood started porcelain production under his own name in Burslem in 1759. Josiah Wedgwood V was Managing Director of the firm from 1930 until 1968 and credited with turning the company's fortunes around. He was responsible for moving production to a modern purpose built factory in a rural setting at Barlaston. It was built between 1938 and 1940. Following years of financial problems at group level, and after various mergers, Wedgwood was placed into administration on a "going concern" basis, in 2009, with 1,800 employees remaining. Private equity firm KPS Capital Partners bought the firm, which included various foreign assets, and some 1,500 jobs were cut in the U.K., more production being transferred to Indonesia, leaving only 800 workers in the U.K. producing the high-end Wedgwood products. Wedgwood station was opened on the 1st January 1940 to serve the Wedgwood complex. In 2003 the line through the station was temporarily closed in connection with the West Coast Main Line modernisation scheme, but on completion the station was not re-opened although the tracks through the station are still regularly used, but trains just pass through. A bus service is provided by Bakers Coaches, not from the station but from Old Road Bridge, a short distance away. The bus service appears in GB Rail Timetable. So much for temporary closure.

Amidst the gloom there is a survivor in the shape of the Rolls Royce name This is despite going into administrative receivership, followed by nationalisation and then privatisation in 1987. In 1884, Henry Royce started an electrical and mechanical business. He made his first car, a two-cylinder Royce 10, in his Manchester factory in 1904, and was introduced to Charles Rolls at the Midland Hotel in Manchester on 14th May of that year. Rolls was proprietor of an early motor car dealership, C.S. Rolls & Co. in Fulham, and in an agreement of 23rd December 1904 Rolls agreed to take all the cars Royce could make. All would be badged as Rolls-Royces, and be sold exclusively by Rolls. With the outbreak of the 1st World War Rolls-Royce was involved with aero engine production. Motor car production was hived off but aero engine manufacture continued, which includes Concorde's engines and engines for the latest Boeing 787 Dreamliner. With a workforce of over 11,000 people, Derby has the largest concentration of Rolls-Royce employees in the UK.

J. Lyons & Co. was a restaurant-chain, with its well known Corner House "Nippy Maids" and also included food-manufacturing, hotel conglomerate, and surprisingly between 1951 and 1963 a computer manufacturer, based on the system that they had used in their business. They also provided outside catering for major event such as racing at Ascot. It was founded in 1887 and Joseph Nathaniel Lyons was appointed to run the company, which was named after him. The company was losing money in the 1960s but it was not acquired until 1978 by Allied Breweries. It became part of the resulting Allied Lyons which also fell on hard economic times in the late 1980s; and was sold, eventually being broken up. Lyons is one of the current Support Brand of Premier Foods Group Ltd., whatever that means.

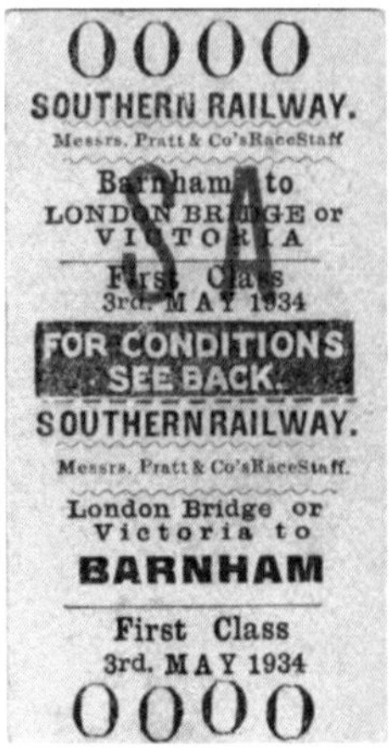


Staying with racecourses we come to Pratt & Co whose early history is unclear. The destination of Barnham is explained by being the station for Fontwell Park race course. On race days a shuttle operates between the station and the race course. The ticket is dated 1934 but I cannot find any other reference to connect Pratt to the racecourse until 1989 when several planning applications were in Pratt's name. It would appear that they were at least managers if not owners of the course. The latest planning application that I could find bearing Pratts name was in 1996 after which Northern Racing's name was on several planning applications when they became owners of the racecourse and subsequently owned or operated ten racecourses. The group was one of the first racecourse concerns to negotiate directly with the bookmaking industry to secure a deal for transmitting pictures from their racecourses directly to Britain's betting shops, and later internationally.

Still with racing there is the Tote's staff to consider. The Racehorse Betting Control Board was created by the Racecourse Betting Act 1928, as a statutory corporation. It was set up by Winston Churchill as a government-appointed board, with the intention of providing a safe, state-controlled alternative to illegal off course bookmakers and ensuring that some gambling revenues were put back into the sport of horse racing. Under the Betting Levy Act 1961 the board was reconstituted as the Horserace Totalisator Board (*the Tote*), with responsibility for the redistribution of funds to racing, which was transferred to the Horserace Betting Levy Board. Privatisation was first suggested in 1989 by the then Conservative government but it took until June 2011 for the industry to be privatised when it was announced that Betfred had been chosen by Culture Secretary Jeremy Hunt as the successful bidder, for a reported figure of £265 million.

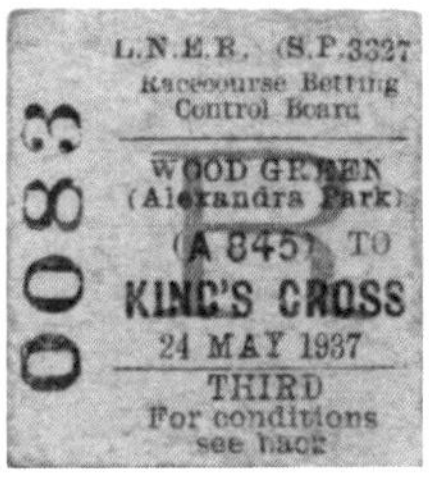


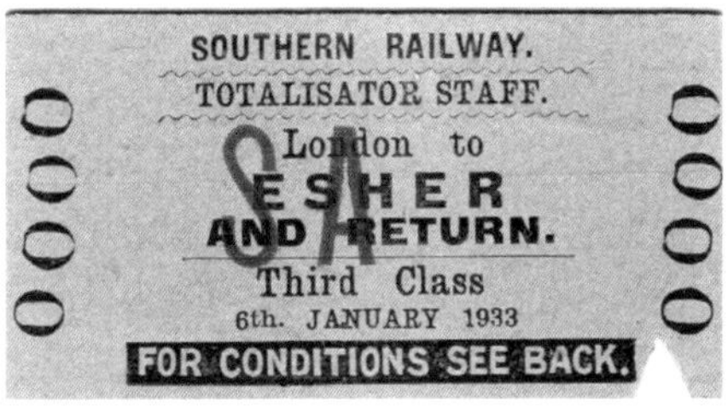


Many of the Workmen's tickets were for transport to and from collieries, in this case a roll ticket of V. & M. Coaches from Grendon to Ansley Hall Colliery.

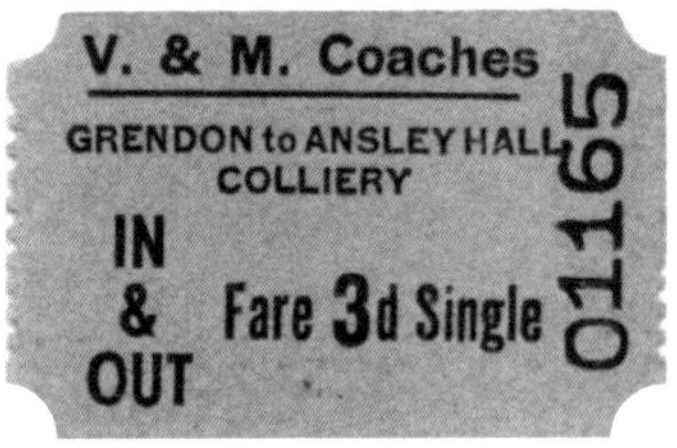


Collieries were not the only destination for contract services as is evidenced by this Daily Work Ticket of Tonna Luxury Coaches Ltd. which is to the Swansea Driver and Vehicle Licensing Centre, now the Driver and Vehicle Licensing Agency. It is not just the private sector that likes rebranding itself.

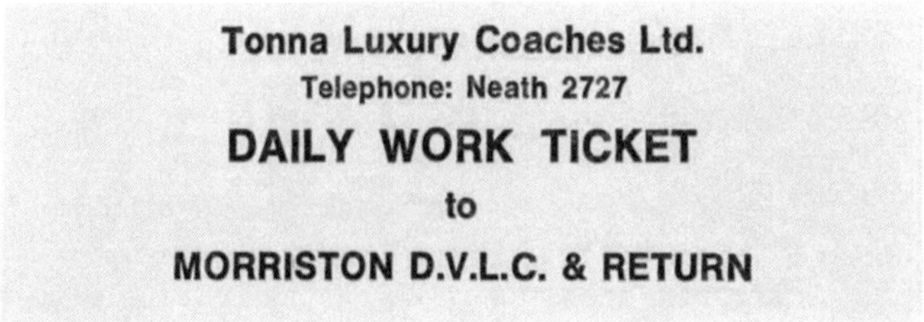

The Sellafield site began life as a wartime ordnance factory. It became Windscale and Calder Works under the UKAEA, with four Calder Hall reactors, the Windscale AGR and infamous piles and various processing facilities. Most of it was taken over by the newly-formed British Nuclear Fuels Ltd in 1971 and the whole site was renamed Sellafield in 1981. Ownership was transferred to the Nuclear Decommissioning Authority in 2005 with operation by Sellafield Ltd. Much of the site is now being decommissioned, including the reactors. The pass was subject to special Travel Scheme arranged by the Cumberland Motor Services for BNFL Sellafield workers.

Rather than paper tickets the colliery transport frequently used plastic or brass tokens. This is a selection of Booth & Fisher colliery tokens.

| | | |
|---|---|---|
| HM | = | High Moor. |
| KP | = | Kiveton Park, (closed 1994) |
| OC | = | Oxcroft an open cast mine, (closed in 2006) and |
| RPK | = | Renishaw Park colliery (1860/1989) |

There is also one from Mrs. E. Flint's service to Glapwell Colliery (closed 1974), hence FLINT GLAP

Tokens were not the exclusive territory of the services to the collieries. Grimsby – Cleethorpes Transport in conjunction with John Sutcliffe Consolidated Stevedores Ltd. used them for Grimsby Immingham return, specified on the other side of the token as well as for the British Transport Dock Board. They were also used on services for the National Dock Labour Board. The 3½d green token is for the North Eastern Gas Board and is valid between 8.00am – 12 NOON and 1.00pm – 5.00pm. It would seem that everything stopped for lunch. Tokens survived decimalisation as evidence by this 3p brass token for Derby Corporation Omnibus Department Employees. The last item is a Yorkshire Traction Co. Ltd employees' brass pass used from the 1930's.

N.D.L.B.

B.T.D.B.

N.E.G.B.

J.S.C.S.

Mine Workers' transport was not the prerogative of road transport and illustrated are three tickets from the Kent coal field. Coal was discovered in East Kent in 1890 when boring for an early Channel Tunnel project. Twelve collieries were reduced to just four after the 1st World War. The geology of the area was not favourable and these four closed between 1969 and 1989.

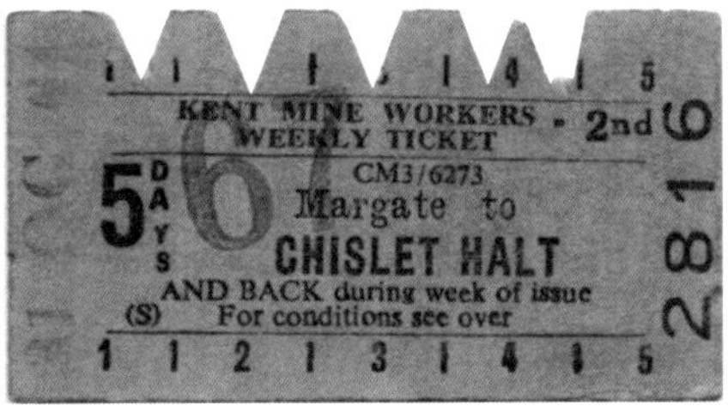


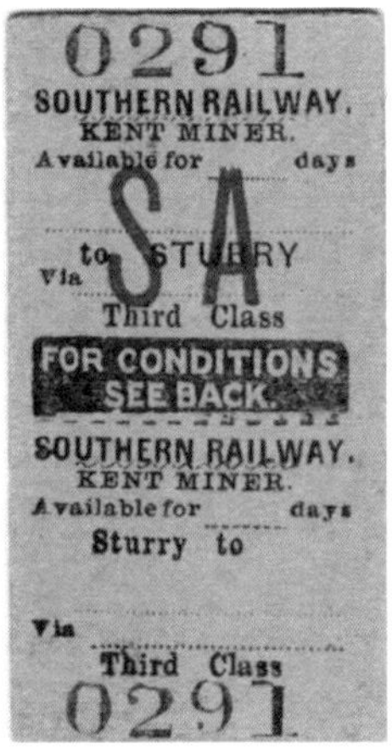


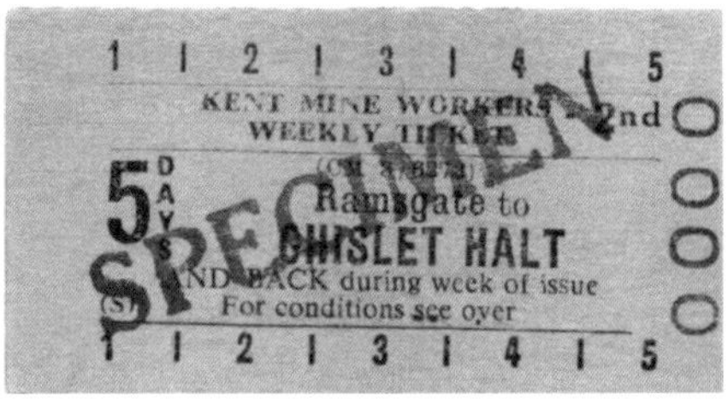


Kent is often referred to as the Garden of England and is famous for hops and fruit. Hop picking was part holiday for the women in the household and their children and part work. Stripping the vines was certainly hard work but was the only time that many of the pickers saw the countryside. Their menfolk might come down from London at the end of their working week. Special trains were put on for the hop pickers and their belongings. The Southern Railway ticket is for the 1938 season. The last hop pickers train from London Bridge to Bodiam ran in September 1958.

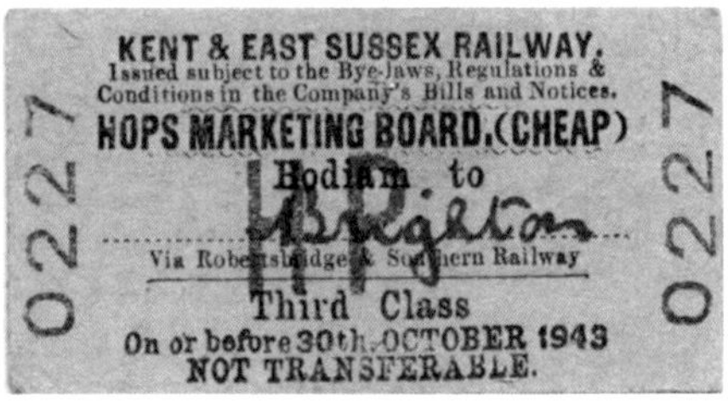


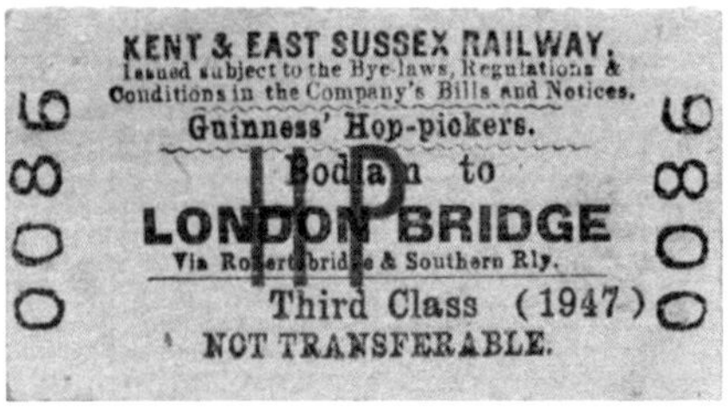

Kent and Sussex were not the only hop and fruit tree areas. The Great Western ticket brackets the two together, while the British Railways one is exclusively Fruit Pickers in the 1953 season. Nowadays there are many contract harvestmen using high tech combine harvesters that smaller farmers could not afford to own for the limited period of use that they would get out of it. There always have been contract harvestmen as harvesting was traditionally a labour intensive job with little mechanisation. The Harvestmen ticket may have a blank destination but the routing via Holyhead & Kingstown (Dun Laoghaire) was for one of the many Irish workers who came to this country for the season.

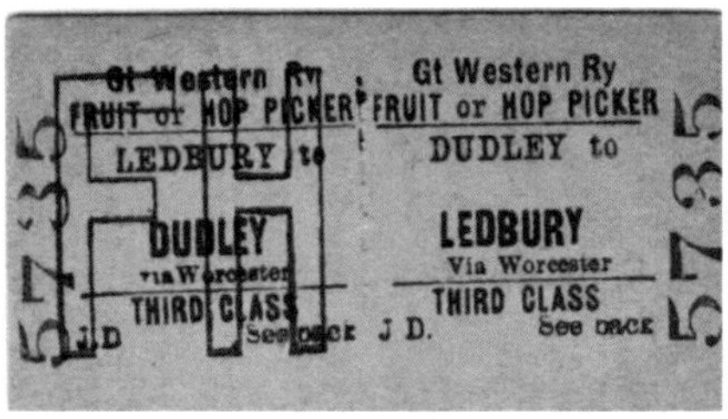


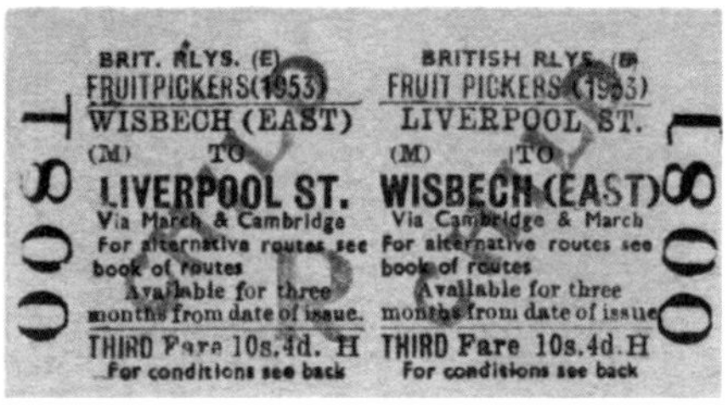


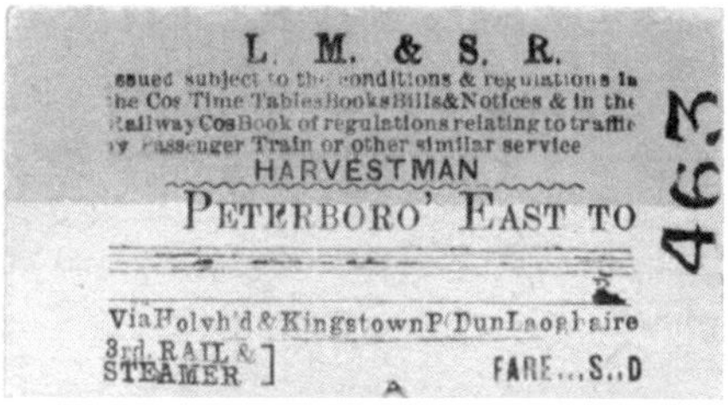


Other itinerant workers were the Fisher Girls who followed the herring fishing fleets as they pursued the shoals as the fish moved down the coast. The lassies were given a modest signing on fee, rail fare and travelling box labels but had to provide their own clothes and a sharp knife.

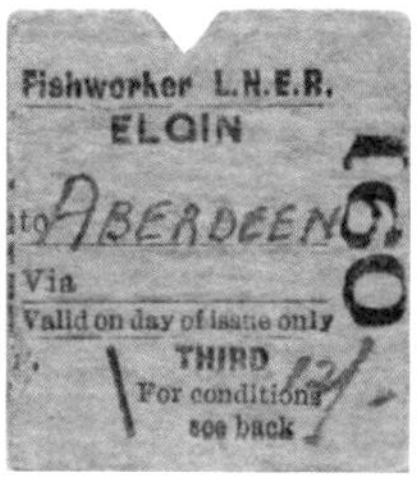


The Festiniog Railway is the oldest surviving railway company in the world having been formed in 1832. Its fortunes waned when the demand for slate fell and tourist travel was insufficient to retain it. Slate traffic ceased in 1939 and the line became derelict. Three workmen's tickets from the era of quarry operations.

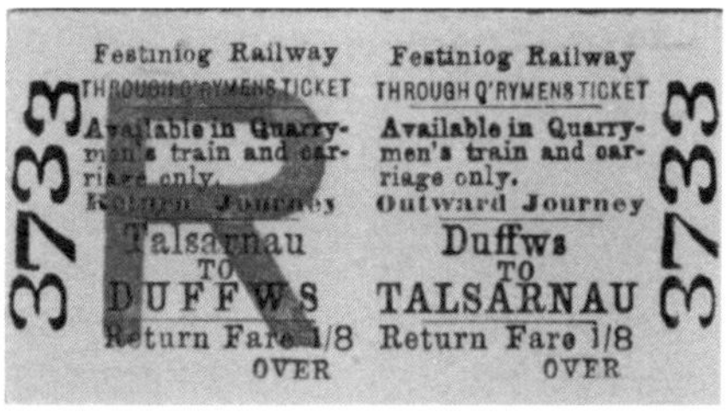


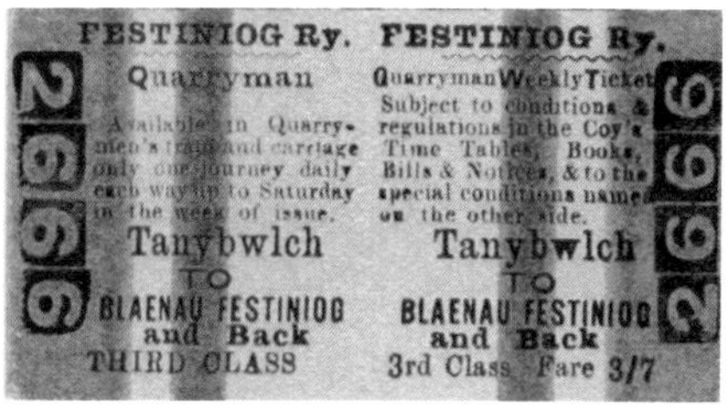


The one overprinted "LAD" reminds us that in the Industrial Revolution it was not only men who worked in dangerous areas but women and children were also working in mines and in factories with unguarded machinery. They started young, as early as 15 years of age, training for a career in the Royal Navy. The LNER ticket is for a Training Ship Boy under 16 Years. The BTC one is just for an R.N. Boy of unspecified age and the two Railway Executive ones are for 16 and 17 year old boys. They had all been connected with HMS Ganges, a training establishment set up in 1865, and after many wanderings and concentration on shore based facilities had arrived at Shotley – under 10 miles from the centre of Ipswich - in 1906. The establishment was closed on 6th June 1976.

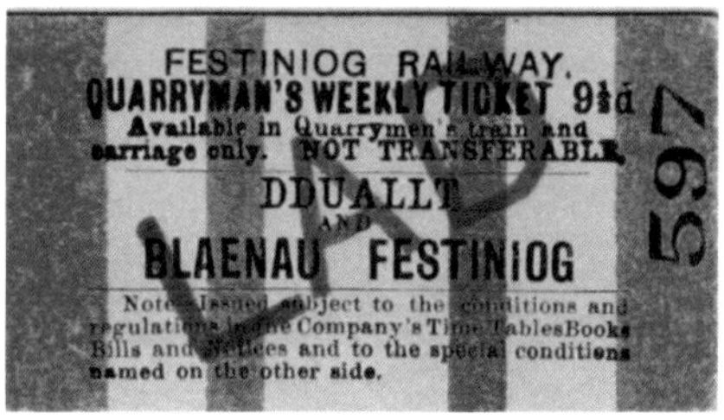


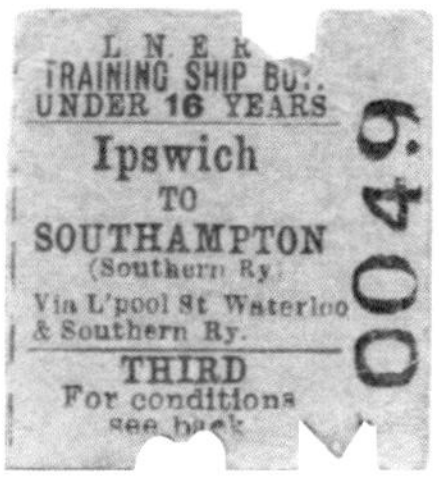


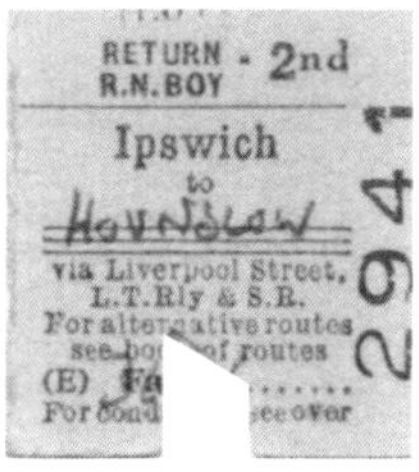


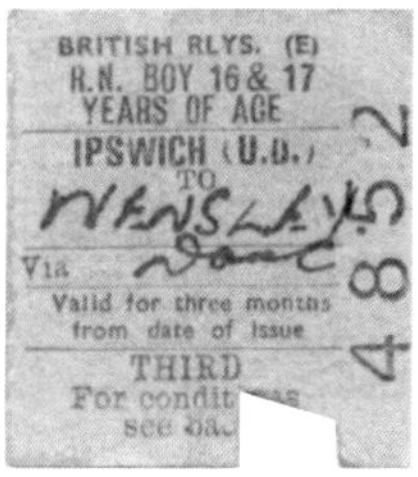


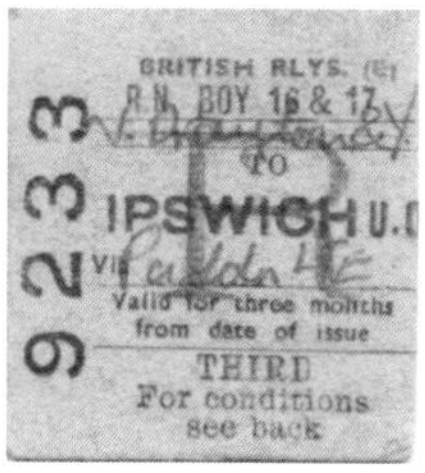

Stanlow & Thornton railway station is located within the Stanlow Refinery in Cheshire. The station is surrounded by the refinery site, so most station users are refinery employees or their sub contractors. The station was opened on 23rd December 1940 jointly by the Great Western Railway and the London, Midland and Scottish Railway. The refinery is the second largest after the Fawley refinery. In 2010, Royal Dutch Shell declared their desire to sell off their refineries in Europe to concentrate on emerging markets in Asia and the Middle East. Stanlow was sold by Shell to Essar Energy for approximately £814 million in 2011.

The London Underground celebrated its 150th anniversary last year while the Singer Manufacturing Company had reached that milestone in 2011 with Isaac Singer's patent on the first practical sewing machine. By 1880 machines with electric motors became available. To meet growing demand in Europe, between 1882 and 1884 Singer built what was then the largest sewing machine factory in the world in Kilbowie. At one time the factory employed 12,000 workers. It closed in 1980 and the Clydebank Business Park was later established on the site of the factory. Singer still exists being part of Kohlberg & Company, an American private equity firm, who bought them in 2004.

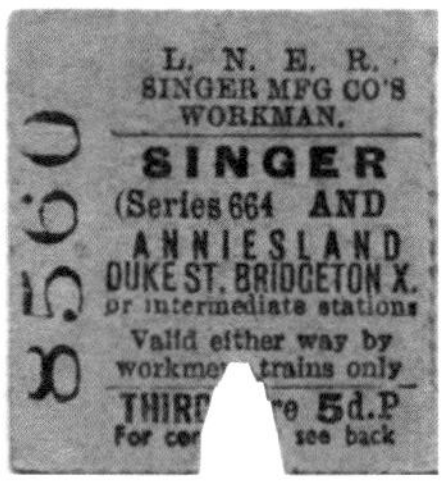


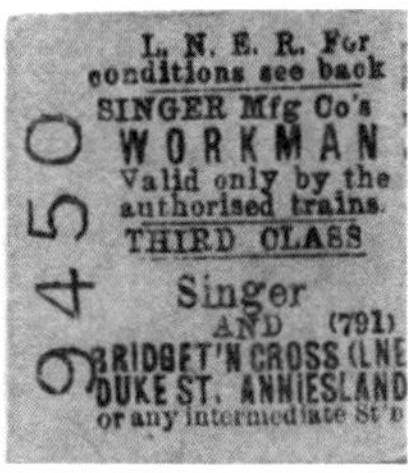


South Coast Garages was established in Lymington before the First World War. Following a change of ownership the company diversified into the mass production of piston rings. The name of the Company was changed to Wellworthy - the original factory standing on a well and a "worthy" being the Wessex name for a ring around a well. Ampress Farm, was bought by Wellworthy in 1939. It was 35 acres in size including large sports grounds. By 1986 the Stanford Road site in Lymington had been closed and the Ampress site has become the head office. At that time the company had 2,500 workers at the plant. Ampress Halt station dates from 1956 and was intended for the use of workers at the nearby Wellworthy factory. It closed in 1989 when the factory closed.

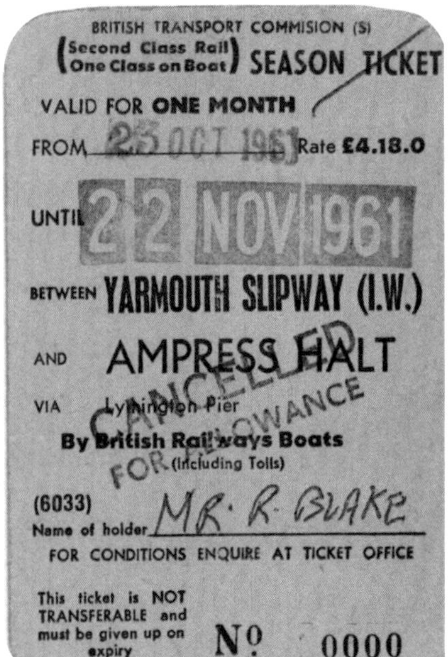


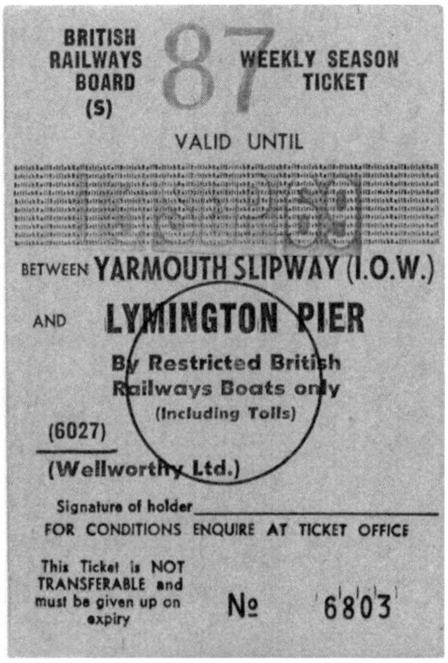

W.D. & H.O. Wills was founded by Henry Overton Wills in 1786, some time after he had moved from Salisbury to Bristol, and went into partnership with Samuel Watkins. Their first shop was in Castle Street but by 1791 the firm had moved to 112 Redcliff Street. Cigarettes first rolled off a new production line at Wills Tobacco's state-of-the-art Hartcliffe factory in 1974, after the company moved its processing plants from Bedminster and Ashton. The Board at Wills believed this modern, efficient factory would produce cigarettes for decades to come but this was not to be with falling sales at a time of greater health awareness and increased duty on tobacco sales. In 1986 Imperial Tobacco, the owners of Wills was bought by the Hanson Trust which culminated with the head office at Hartcliffe closing in 1989, followed by the transfer of cigarette manufacturing from Hartcliffe to Nottingham in 1990. (3042A) denotes that the ticket was issued from British Railway's Oxford Street office.

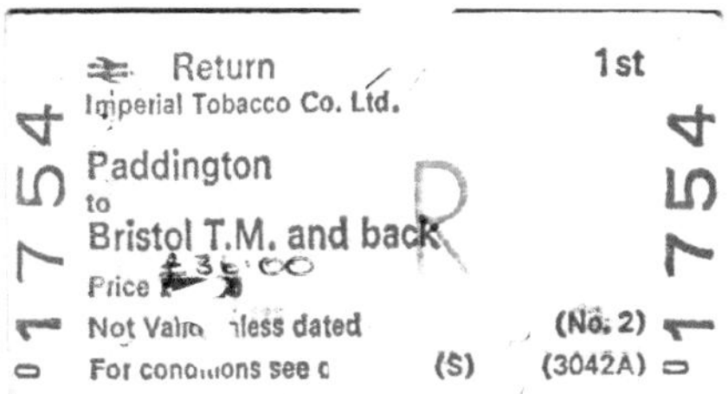


Knowle Hospital was built in 1830 as the Hampshire County Lunatic Asylum. It ended its days as a National Health Service mental hospital housing about 400 mentally ill patients. Many new buildings had been added over the years, such as nurses' homes, open accommodation for patients and an education and assessment centre. There were also playing fields, a swimming pool and a church which were open for public use. The hospital closed in 1996.

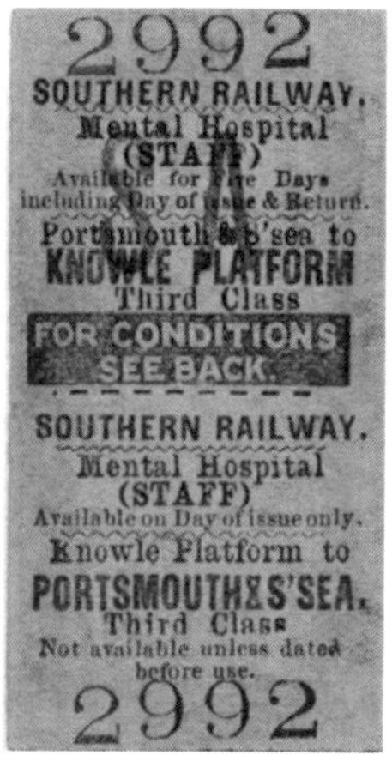


While on a medical theme, a couple of offerings from the Southern Railway an Ambulance for one company's employee and One Railway Convalescent Home Patient.

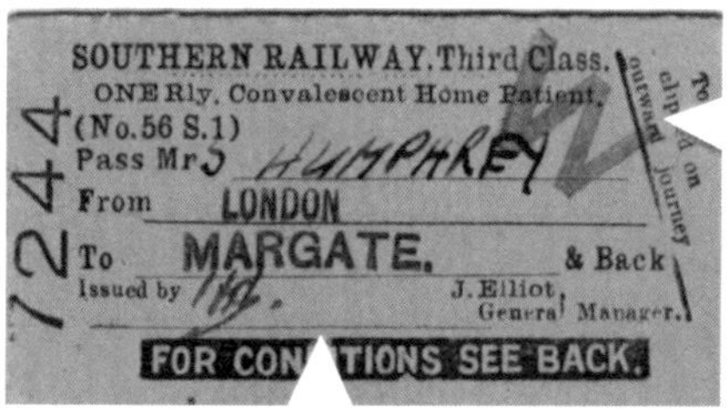


Keeping with the Southern Railway we find One Company's Employee from the London Central Division being sent on a staff Educational Class in Brighton. The British Railways one is for One Employee to attend a Safety on Electrified Lines Film Show in June 1963. Electrification was going on in Glasgow in the early 1960s and this ticket dates from two to three years after the introduction of the Glasgow Blue Trains.

While the previous items have been largely for manual workers special tickets existed for outdoor events and artists behind the footlights. Repertory companies, orchestras and the like needed to move all their props, musical instruments, cast and crew from one venue to the next. Rail travel was the answer. The tickets for specified organisations were made up into a pack with a separate ticket for each leg of the journey. The British Transport Commission Circular Tour for Sadlers Wells Opera Co consisted of ten individual tickets but the total length of the tour is not known as they are all dated April 17th, 1960. Apart from these customised tickets there were generic series such as that used by the Southern Railway. Now the companies have customised lorries which can handle all the sets, staging etc. and transport it from stage door to stage door with high quality coaches to carry performers and crew to their next venue.

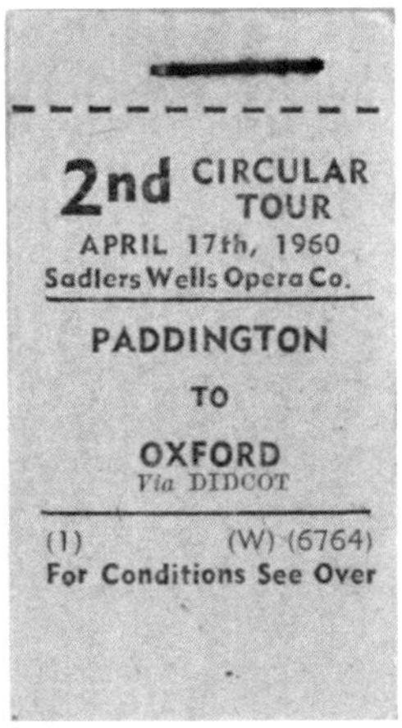


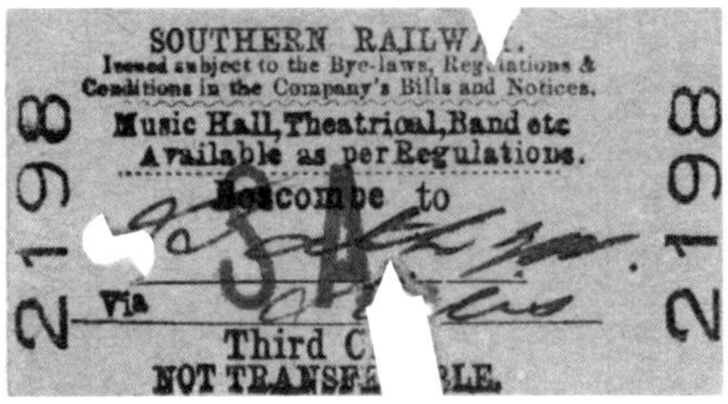

We have been looking at workers travelling to a particular place of work but for some it is just the start of the day as driving is their occupation. The Tilbury - Gravesend ferry has an ancient pedigree with records showing its existence by at least 1571. In 1927 car ferries were introduced. Car Ferry is a bit of a misnomer as tickets were produced for a variety of vehicles. The vehicle ferry stopped running in 1964 as a result of the Dartford Tunnel opening in 1963. What would toll collectors of today think of a Hand Barrow with two wheels?

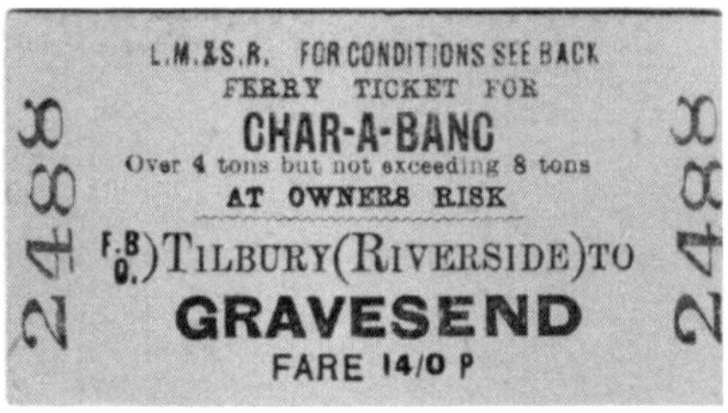


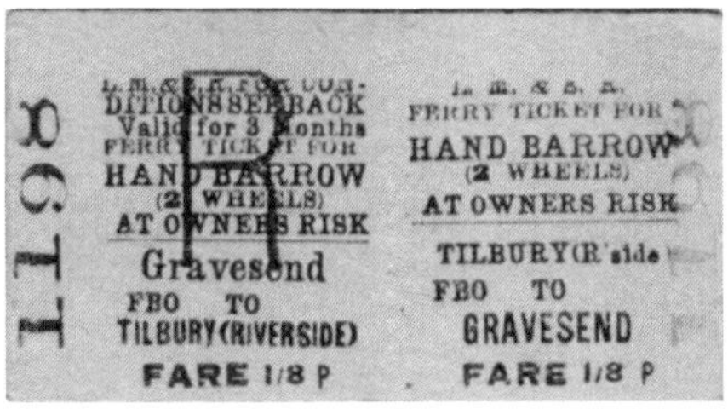


There was a Black Market in prepaid vouchers, well perhaps Black Market is a bit strong. Lorry and coach drivers were known to use the free Blackwall Tunnel rather than Dartford and sell the vouchers, provided by their employers, at a discount to other drivers. I am sure that this practice was not in the authorities minds when they produced the vouchers. THIS TICKET IS TRANSFERABLE. Dart Tags have taken away the possibility of pecuniary benefit and the Global Positioning System (GPS) has meant that transport managers can see precisely where all their vehicles are.

The River Humber's ferry service between Hull and New Holland ended with the opening of the Humber Bridge 24th June 1981. In most cases a new bridge, such as the Humber Bridge, or tunnel, such as Dartford kill off the ferry. However the coming of "Le Shuttle" has not killed off the short sea route ferries from Dover or Newhaven etc.

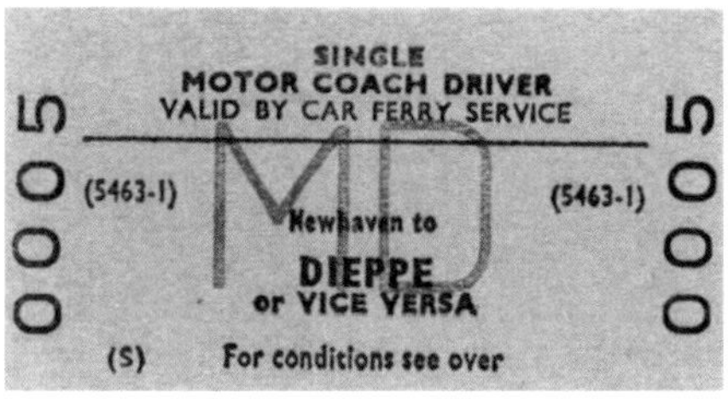

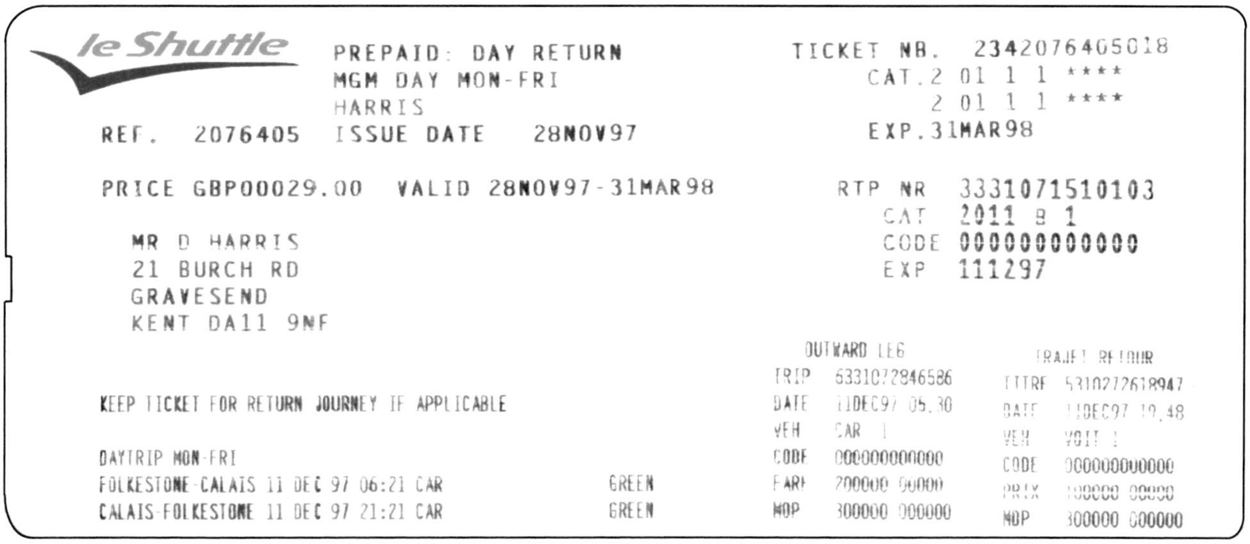


*[actual size 203mm x 83mm]*

Over the years attempts have been made to stagger the rush hour by providing cheap Early Morning tickets.

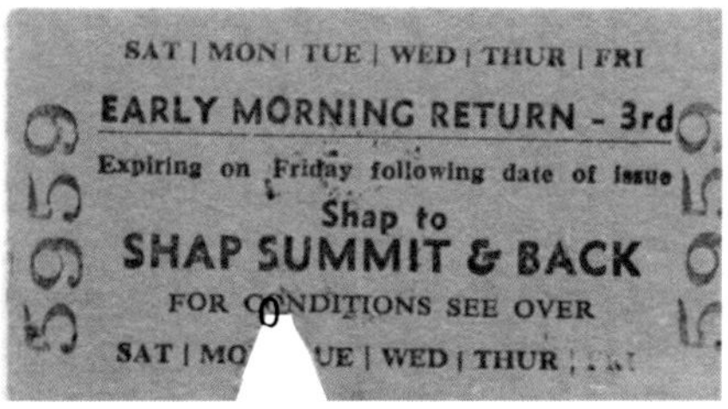


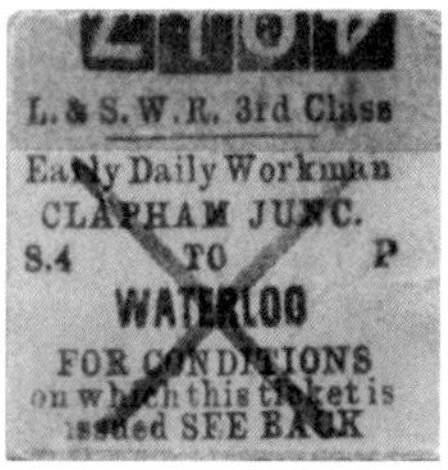


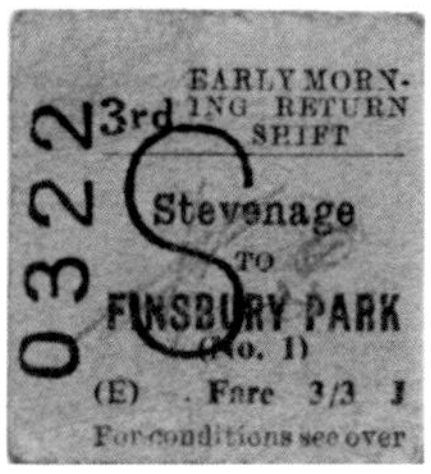


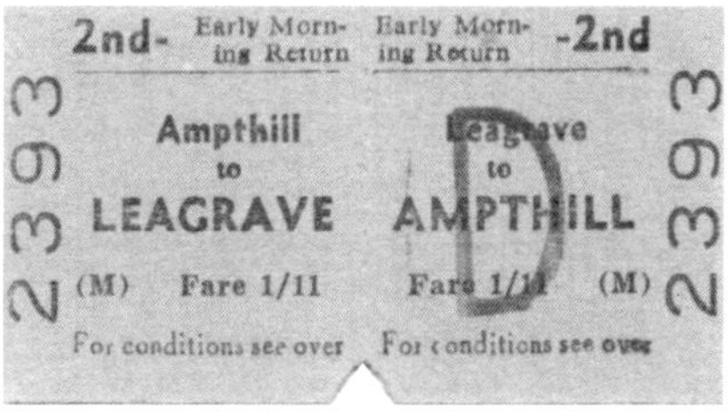

The South Eastern Division offered "Early Bird" season tickets from Gravesend and Meopham, which is carried on by SouthEastern for 7 day and monthly season tickets. I could not find any reference on the SouthEastern website to this facility but there is reference on the *railsaver* website. These season tickets are easily recognisable being blue with red text.

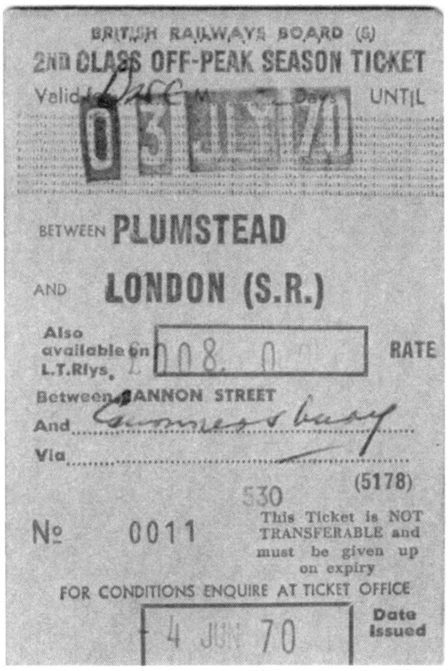


There were also off peak seasons, which may still be available from an extremely limited number of stations.

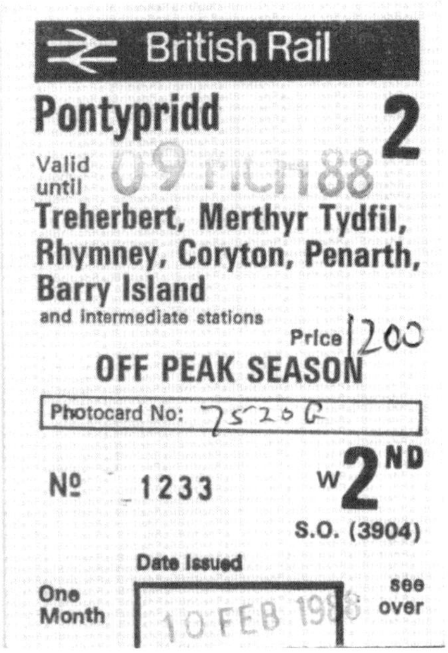

Having promoted cheap early morning tickets for many years there began moves to not only abolish these fares but charge higher fares in the morning peak, which usually means up to 9.30am Transport for London also discovered an earlier practice, from British Railways Board (BRB) days, whereby there were restrictions on the use of cheap day returns on evening rush hour trains, and TfL charge a higher evening rush hour cash and Oyster fare. Day Off Peak Travelcards once having complied with the morning restrictions are not surcharged for use during the evening rush hour.

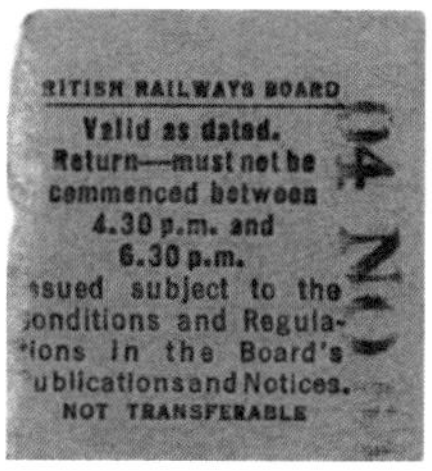


Anglia had a different approach to commuters with their Commuter Club. There is no reference to it in the current franchisee's web site but there was a description of it in response to complaints at fares increases in the Ipswich Star in December 2001. An Anglia spokesman said that they were trying to realign the fares to make them viable. He went on to comment that the Commuter Club was introduced two years earlier as a package of measures including seat reservation and automatic payments if trains run more than 30 minutes late. The Anglia franchise came to an end in 2004 and I could not find any later references to the Commuter Club.

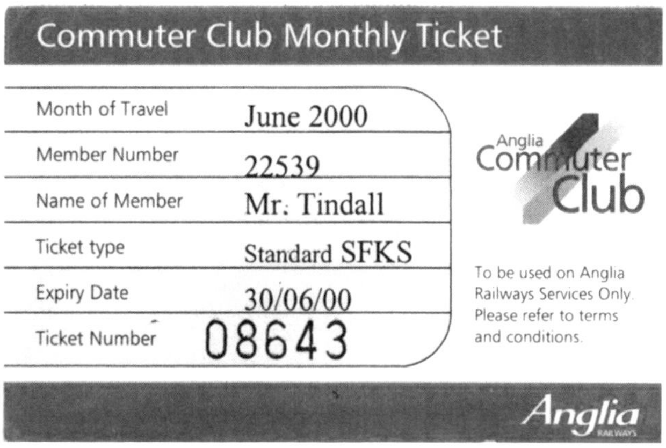


During May 1972 an electronic ticket system was introduced between Glasgow Central, Gourock and Wemyss Bay. There were twenty-five different types of tickets designed for the scheme. The oxide backed tickets did not specifically differentiate between pleasure travel and commuting. However, the higher the number of stored journeys the more likely was their use by commuters rather than leisure travellers. Of the types of tickets involved, Day and Period return tickets were only issued to and from Ayrshire stations, while two, ten, twenty and fifty journey tickets were only used on the Gourock and Wemyss Bay lines. Their use officially came to an end after 13th October 1979 although yellow tickets were still being used after that date until ticket stocks were replenished in the normal way.

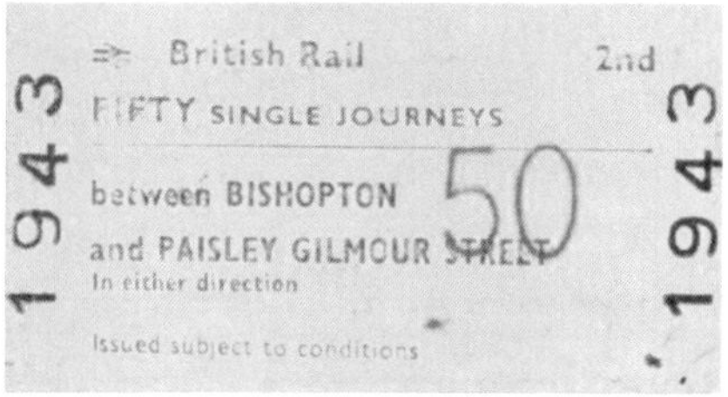


London Underground had experimented with Edmondson sized oxide backed tickets and longer season tickets, but the Underground ultimately standardised on a system with credit card sized tickets.

Commercial Travellers were travelling representatives/salesmen, not of the door to door variety, but a link between the manufacturer/supplier and the wholesalers/shops. Before the increase in car ownership Commercial Travellers relied heavily on the railways both to enable them to move around their area, and then to return home for the weekend. Ticket 489 is a little odd as it provides for the return the day following the day of issue by certain trains only.

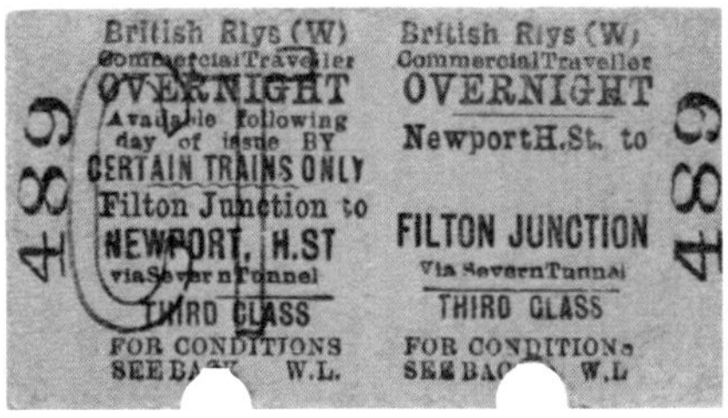

We met the Commercial Traveller earlier with his certificate of identity and vouchers for travel to and from his home station at weekend and these are some of the tickets that would have been available on production of the certificate. While all the return halves provide the same period of validity how that was expressed varied from company to company.

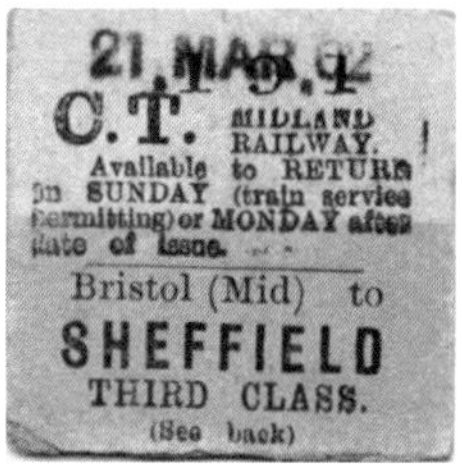

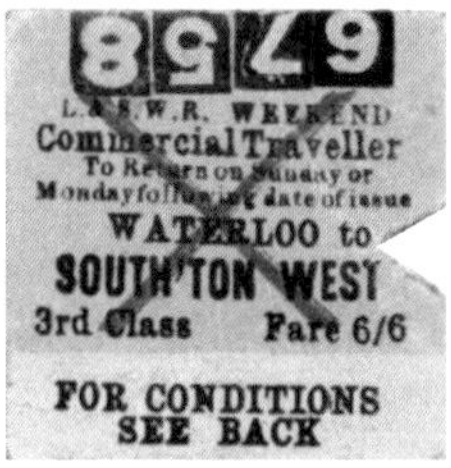


A step, or several steps, up from the Commercial Traveller is the Traders/Business Ticket. These were generally limited to a named person and specified the position they held in the company. Setting out the routes and stations to and at which the season ticket was valid often led to a lengthy insert in a leatherette cover. The BR (M) ticket (shown overleaf) is 12 inches overall in length. For durability the insert is on linen rather than paper. The subsequent SR ticket is by comparison 9 inches whereas the LMS one is a mere 6¼ inches.

Mr. Sloane, Mr. Apps and Mr Hosking must have had a good grasp of the railway system to know exactly what was included and what was excluded.

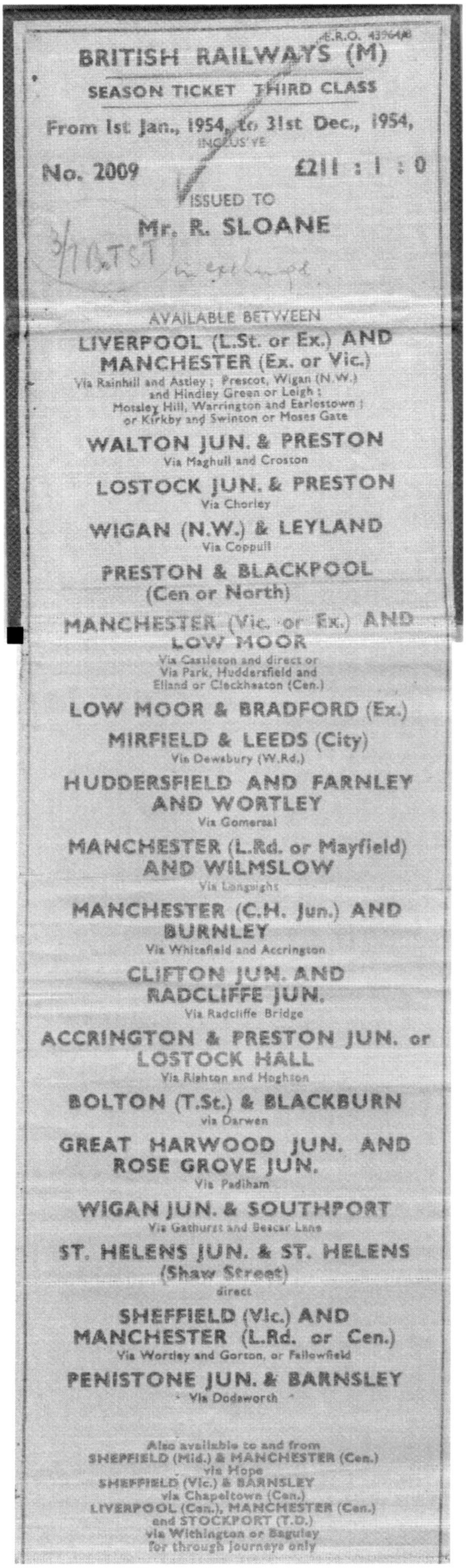

E.R.O. 43964/8

BRITISH RAILWAYS (M)

SEASON TICKET THIRD CLASS

From 1st Jan., 1954, to 31st Dec., 1954, INCLUSIVE

No. 2009 £211 : 1 : 0

ISSUED TO

Mr. R. SLOANE

AVAILABLE BETWEEN

LIVERPOOL (L.St. or Ex.) AND MANCHESTER (Ex. or Vic.)
Via Rainhill and Astley ; Prescot, Wigan (N.W.) and Hindley Green or Leigh ; Mossley Hill, Warrington and Earlestown ; or Kirkby and Swinton or Moses Gate

WALTON JUN. & PRESTON
Via Maghull and Croston

LOSTOCK JUN. & PRESTON
Via Chorley

WIGAN (N.W.) & LEYLAND
Via Coppull

PRESTON & BLACKPOOL (Cen or North)

MANCHESTER (Vic. or Ex.) AND LOW MOOR
Via Castleton and direct or Via Park, Huddersfield and Elland or Cleckheaton (Cen.)

LOW MOOR & BRADFORD (Ex.)

MIRFIELD & LEEDS (City)
Via Dewsbury (W.Rd.)

HUDDERSFIELD AND FARNLEY AND WORTLEY
Via Gomersal

MANCHESTER (L.Rd. or Mayfield) AND WILMSLOW
Via Longsight

MANCHESTER (C.H. Jun.) AND BURNLEY
Via Whitefield and Accrington

CLIFTON JUN. AND RADCLIFFE JUN.
Via Radcliffe Bridge

ACCRINGTON & PRESTON JUN. or LOSTOCK HALL
Via Rishton and Hoghton

BOLTON (T.St.) & BLACKBURN
via Darwen

GREAT HARWOOD JUN. AND ROSE GROVE JUN.
Via Padiham

WIGAN JUN. & SOUTHPORT
Via Gathurst and Bescar Lane

ST. HELENS JUN. & ST. HELENS (Shaw Street)
direct

SHEFFIELD (Vic.) AND MANCHESTER (L.Rd. or Cen.)
Via Wortley and Gorton, or Fallowfield

PENISTONE JUN. & BARNSLEY
Via Dodworth

Also available to and from
SHEFFIELD (Mid.) & MANCHESTER (Cen.)
via Hope
SHEFFIELD (Vic.) & BARNSLEY
via Chapeltown (Cen.)
LIVERPOOL (Cen.), MANCHESTER (Cen.) and STOCKPORT (T.D.)
via Withington or Baguley
for through journeys only

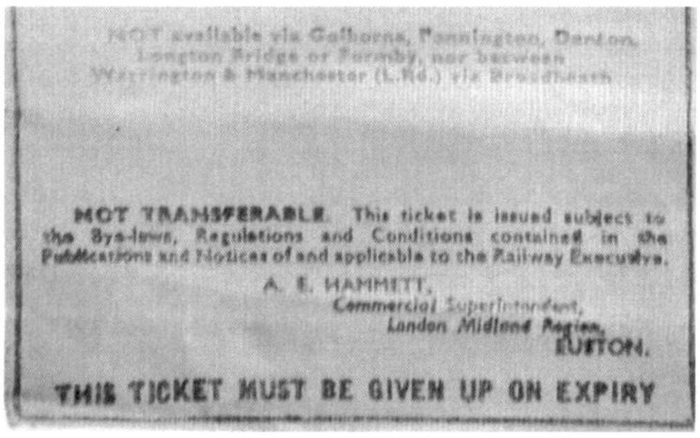

NOT available via Garston, Pennington, Denton, Longton Bridge or Formby, nor between Warrington & Manchester (L.Rd.) via Broadheath

NOT TRANSFERABLE. This ticket is issued subject to the Bye-laws, Regulations and Conditions contained in the Publications and Notices of and applicable to the Railway Executive.

A. E. HAMMETT,
*Commercial Superintendent,*
*London Midland Region,*
EUSTON.

THIS TICKET MUST BE GIVEN UP ON EXPIRY

## SOUTHERN RAILWAY

PS ($\frac{5}{4\ 9}$) (212)

**TRADER'S SEASON TICKET—THIRD CLASS.**

**From JUNE 29th, 1949 to DEC. 28th, 1949,**
inclusive.

**No. L1621.**

ISSUED TO
Messrs. GEORGE HARKER & Co., Ltd.,
9, Eastcheap, E.C. 3,
in favour of their Representative,

**Mr. EDWARD MASON APPS.**

AVAILABLE BETWEEN

**CHARING CROSS, CANNON STREET, VICTORIA AND HORLEY**
VIA FOREST HILL, NORBURY and PURLEY.
**LONDON BRIDGE AND BROMLEY NORTH**
**NORWOOD JUNCTION OR SELHURST AND EPSOM OR EPSOM DOWNS**
VIA WALLINGTON and CHEAM.
**SOUTH CROYDON AND DORMANS**
VIA UPPER WARLINGHAM and LINGFIELD.
**PURLEY AND CATERHAM**
**REDHILL AND DORKING TOWN**
VIA REIGATE
**WATERLOO AND HASLEMERE**
VIA WORCESTER PARK, COBHAM or WORPLESDON.
**LEATHERHEAD AND DORKING NORTH**
**CLAPHAM JUNCTION AND ASCOT**
[illegible] EGHAM.
**MALDEN AND TWICKENHAM**
VIA KINGSTON.
**WEYBRIDGE AND VIRGINIA WATER**
VIA CHERTSEY.
**WOKING AND FARNHAM**
VIA ASH VALE.
**ASH VALE AND ASCOT**
VIA CAMBERLEY.
**GUILDFORD AND CRANLEIGH**

Also available to and from
LONDON BRIDGE or BALHAM and SUTTON
via Carshalton.
WIMBLEDON and WEST CROYDON
via Beddington Lane.
BARNES and FELTHAM
via Hounslow.
DORKING TOWN and GUILDFORD
via Gomshall.
GUILDFORD and ALDERSHOT
via Ash,
for through journeys only.

**NOT via DENMARK HILL, CRYSTAL PALACE, CATFORD BRIDGE, HAYDONS ROAD, ST. HELIER, BLACKWATER, HORSHAM, THREE BRIDGES or EAST GRINSTEAD.**

This ticket is not transferable, and is issued and accepted upon the condition that the Trader and the Holder are subject to the Conditions contained in the form of application, and to the Conditions and Regulations in the Company's Bills and Notices, and in the Railway Companies' Book of Regulations relating to Traffic by Passenger train or other similar service.

Rate £54 : 1 : 0

JOHN ELLIOT,
*General Manager.*

**THIS TICKET MUST BE GIVEN UP ON EXPIRY.**

## London Midland and Scottish
**RAILWAY COMPANY.**

**TRADER'S SEASON TICKET. FIRST CLASS**

**From 1st Oct., 1936, to 30th Sept., 1937,**
INCLUSIVE

**No. D101** **£50 : 7 : 0**

ISSUED TO
Messrs. S. Russell & Sons, Ltd., Bath Lane, Leicester,
for the use of their Director,

**Mr. RANDALL GARFIELD HOSKING**

AVAILABLE BETWEEN

MIDLAND.

**LEICESTER & RUGBY**
Via Ullesthorpe
AND INTERMEDIATE STATIONS
Also available to and from
LEICESTER & ST. PANCRAS
via Kibworth
for through journeys only.

L.&N.W.

**RUGBY & EUSTON**
Via Long Buckby
AND INTERMEDIATE STATIONS
Also available to and from
RUGBY & ROADE
via Weedon
for through journeys only.

L.&N.E.

Also available to and from
RUGBY (Cen.) & LEICESTER (Cen.)
via Main Line
for through journeys only.

This Ticket is **NOT TRANSFERABLE**, and is issued and accepted upon the condition that the Trader and the Holder are subject to the Conditions contained in the form of application, and to the Conditions and Regulations in the Companies' Time Tables, Books, Bills and Notices, and in the Railway Companies' Book of Regulations relating to Traffic by Passenger Train or other similar Service.

GLYNNE ROBERTS, *Secretary*,
EUSTON STATION.

*Exd. & Entd.*............................

**THIS TICKET MUST BE GIVEN UP ON EXPIRY.**

Newspaper distribution was often done by rail, in the days when trains had Guards, and guards' vans. I travelled to and from work via Holborn Viaduct station before it was rebuilt. The evening paper vans drove from Fleet Street, just up the road, almost onto the platforms. The guard oversaw the loading of the bundles and threw them out onto the platform at the appropriate station. There was also activity later in the evening when the next morning's first edition daily papers were being handled. The conditions on both these tickets are quite interesting. The journey from Luton is presumably to start work, travelling in an ordinary carriage. It is restricted to returning on the 04.25 train on weekdays. The conditions permit the bearer to travel in a van or other vehicle that does not have passenger accommodation. The conditions of the other ticket restrict its use to travelling exclusively on the business of W.H. Smith. Why such a ticket between two adjacent stations less than a mile apart was required is a mystery.

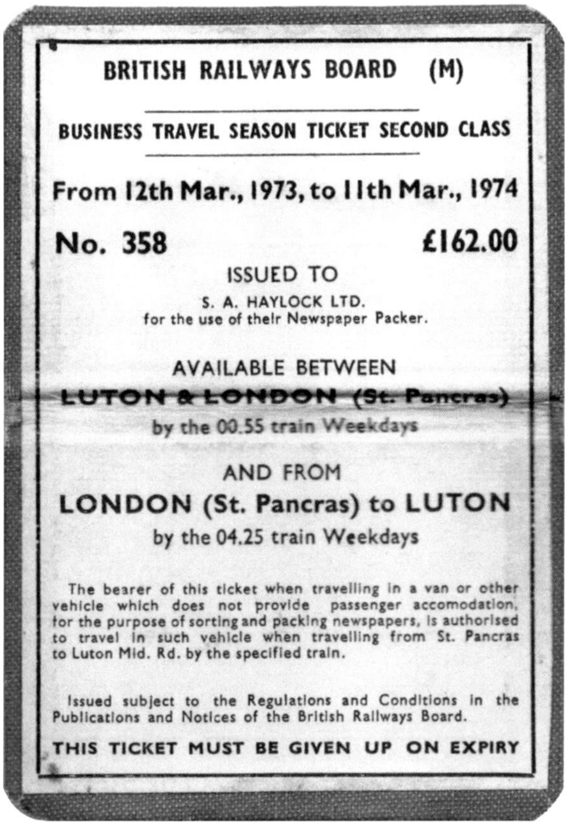
BRITISH RAILWAYS BOARD (M)

BUSINESS TRAVEL SEASON TICKET SECOND CLASS

From 12th Mar., 1973, to 11th Mar., 1974

No. 358 £162.00

ISSUED TO

S. A. HAYLOCK LTD.
for the use of their Newspaper Packer.

AVAILABLE BETWEEN

~~LUTON & LONDON (St. Pancras)~~

by the 00.55 train Weekdays

AND FROM

LONDON (St. Pancras) to LUTON

by the 04.25 train Weekdays

The bearer of this ticket when travelling in a van or other vehicle which does not provide passenger accomodation, for the purpose of sorting and packing newspapers, is authorised to travel in such vehicle when travelling from St. Pancras to Luton Mid. Rd. by the specified train.

Issued subject to the Regulations and Conditions in the Publications and Notices of the British Railways Board.

THIS TICKET MUST BE GIVEN UP ON EXPIRY

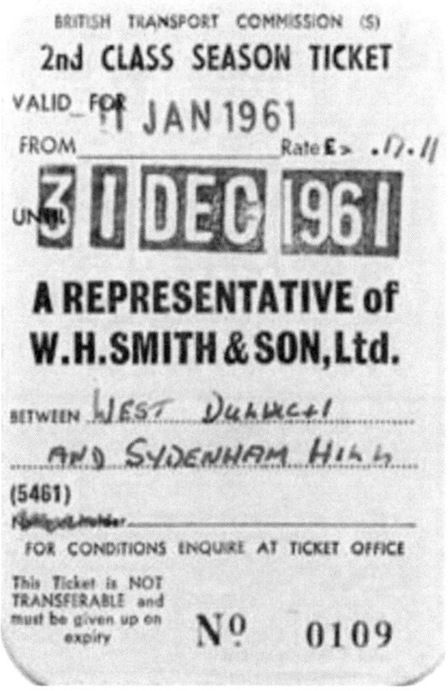
BRITISH TRANSPORT COMMISSION (S)

2nd CLASS SEASON TICKET

VALID FOR 1 JAN 1961
FROM Rate £s .17.11

UNTIL 31 DEC 1961

A REPRESENTATIVE of
W.H.SMITH & SON, Ltd.

BETWEEN WEST DULWICH
AND SYDENHAM HILL

(5461)

FOR CONDITIONS ENQUIRE AT TICKET OFFICE

This Ticket is NOT TRANSFERABLE and must be given up on expiry

Nº 0109

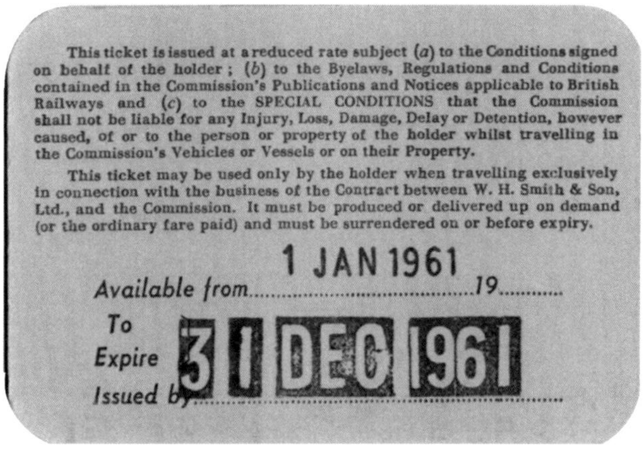
This ticket is issued at a reduced rate subject (*a*) to the Conditions signed on behalf of the holder; (*b*) to the Byelaws, Regulations and Conditions contained in the Commission's Publications and Notices applicable to British Railways and (*c*) to the SPECIAL CONDITIONS that the Commission shall not be liable for any Injury, Loss, Damage, Delay or Detention, however caused, of or to the person or property of the holder whilst travelling in the Commission's Vehicles or Vessels or on their Property.

This ticket may be used only by the holder when travelling exclusively in connection with the business of the Contract between W. H. Smith & Son, Ltd., and the Commission. It must be produced or delivered up on demand (or the ordinary fare paid) and must be surrendered on or before expiry.

*Available from* 1 JAN 1961 *19*
*To Expire* 31 DEC 1961
*Issued by*

Another body that at some time had special tickets and fares was the police force. The North British ticket is dated in 1889 and the Sharpness ticket is dated in 1937. At a later date Metropolitan Police Officers were provided with travel warrants for standard travel ticket. The North British Railway Co. form has space for Shipwrecked Mariners, probably a frequent occurrence in the 1880's.

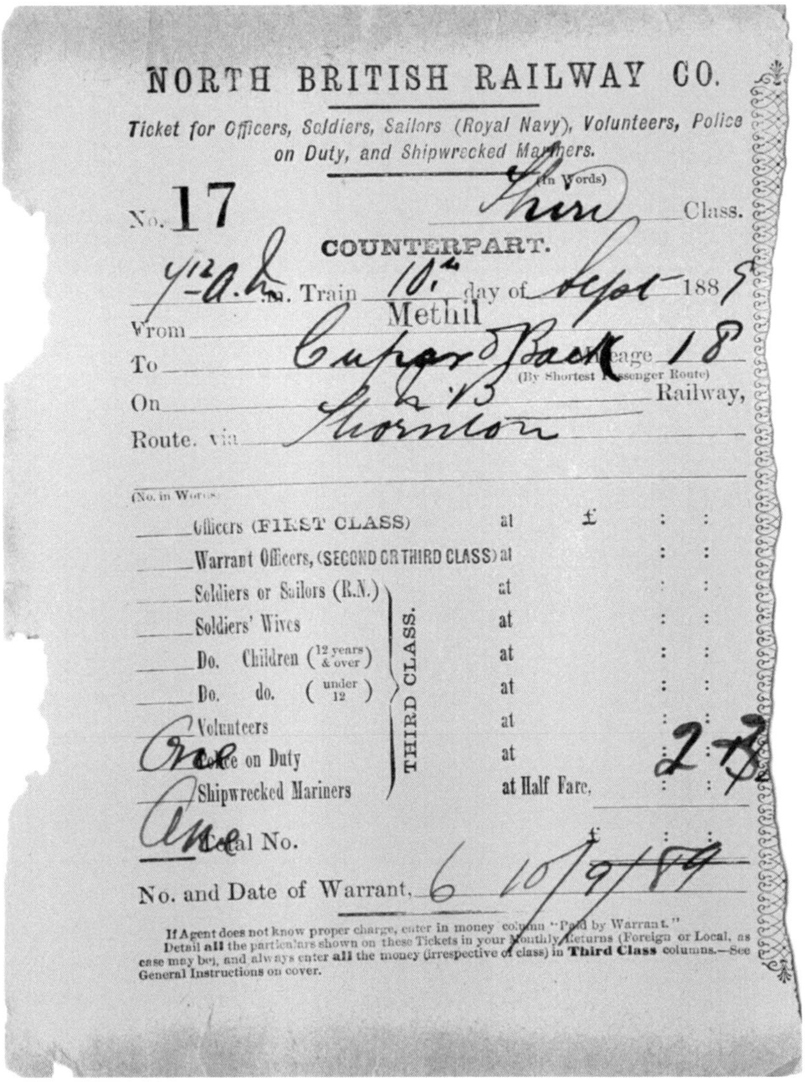

NORTH BRITISH RAILWAY CO.

*Ticket for Officers, Soldiers, Sailors (Royal Navy), Volunteers, Police on Duty, and Shipwrecked Mariners.*

No. 17 ..... (In Words) Three ..... Class.

COUNTERPART.

7-12 a.m. Train 10th day of Sept 1889

From Methil

To Cupar & Back ..... Mileage 18 (By Shortest Passenger Route)

On ..... Railway,

Route, via Thornton

| (No. in Words) | | | | |
|---|---|---|---|---|
| Officers (FIRST CLASS) | at | £ | : | : |
| Warrant Officers, (SECOND OR THIRD CLASS) | at | | : | : |
| Soldiers or Sailors (R.N.) — THIRD CLASS. | at | | : | : |
| Soldiers' Wives | at | | : | : |
| Do. Children (12 years & over) | at | | : | : |
| Do. do. (under 12) | at | | : | : |
| Volunteers | at | | : | : |
| One Police on Duty | at | | 2 | 7 |
| Shipwrecked Mariners | at Half Fare, | | : | : |
| One Total No. | | £ | : | : |

No. and Date of Warrant, 6 10/9/89

If Agent does not know proper charge, enter in money column "Paid by Warrant." Detail all the particulars shown on these Tickets in your Monthly Returns (Foreign or Local, as case may be), and always enter all the money (irrespective of class) in Third Class columns.—See General Instructions on cover.

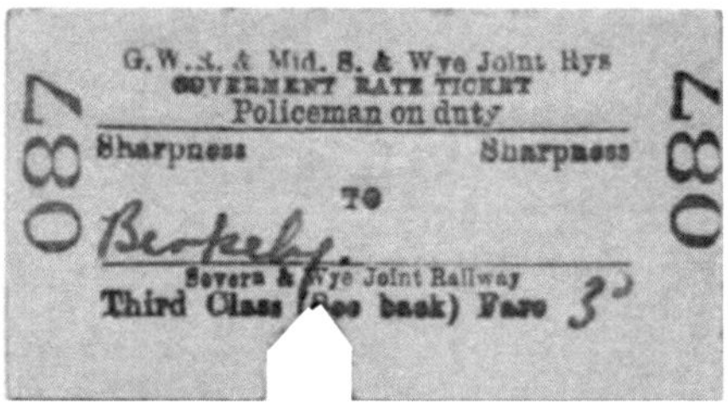

087

G.W.R. & Mid. R. & Wye Joint Rys
GOVERNMENT RATE TICKET
Policeman on duty
Sharpness Sharpness
TO
Berkeley
Severn & Wye Joint Railway
Third Class (See back) Fare 3d

087

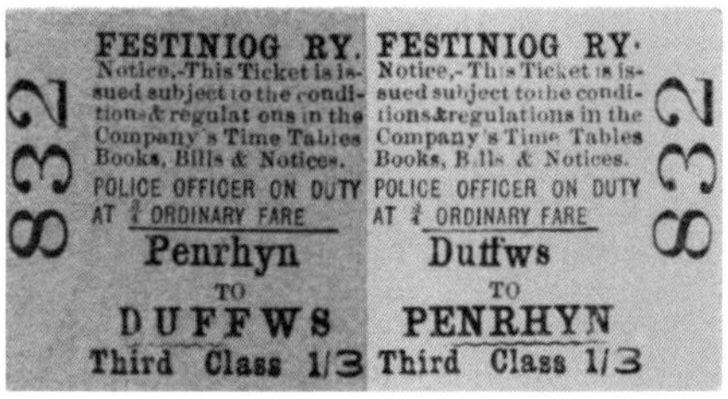

832

| FESTINIOG RY. | FESTINIOG RY. |
|---|---|
| Notice,-This Ticket is issued subject to the conditions & regulations in the Company's Time Tables Books, Bills & Notices. | Notice,-This Ticket is issued subject to the conditions & regulations in the Company's Time Tables Books, Bills & Notices. |
| POLICE OFFICER ON DUTY AT ¾ ORDINARY FARE | POLICE OFFICER ON DUTY AT ¾ ORDINARY FARE |
| Penrhyn TO DUFFWS | Duffws TO PENRHYN |
| Third Class 1/3 | Third Class 1/3 |

832

**METROPOLITAN POLICE TRAVEL WARRANT** – **Fare not payable at time of booking** BR 4402/169

This warrant is not transferable, is valid for 30 days from the date of issue and must be exchanged for a ticket before commencement of travel. Any alterations must be signed by the issuing officer and supported by the Police Force Stamp.

F.I. BRANCH
METROPOLITAN POLICE OFFICE
EASTBURY HOUSE
30–34 ALBERT EMBANKMENT, LONDON SE1 7UD

Code No. 9 6 9 9

FOR OFFICE USE
Issued at:

To: BRITISH RAIL/LONDON TRANSPORT
Please issue without charge to bearer Ann Cameron
tickets as under by the CHEAPEST RECOGNISED ROUTE.

| No. of Passengers (in words) | | Class | Ticket Type |
|---|---|---|---|
| Adults | Children | | |
| 1 | | ~~FIRST~~/SECOND* | SINGLE/~~RETURN/SEASON~~* *Delete as necessary |

JOURNEY DETAILS
FROM Baker Street TO Uxbridge
DATES FROM (OUT) 06-12-85 TO (RETURN) —

Signature of Officer issuing ..... Rank and No. WPC 372
Police Station Paddington Green Date 06-12-85 Police Service Code:

Description of ticket/s
No/s of ticket/s
Route
Date

| Account No | Warrant No. | Amount Payable £ £ £ £ p p | INSERT 1 IF: Season Ticket | 1st Class |
|---|---|---|---|---|
| 2 : 9 6 9 9 ? | ZP 48133 | & | ! | N L |

*[Actual size 195mm x 105mm]*

There is now an agreement with the Association of Train Operating Companies (ATOC) to enable Metropolitan and City of London police officers, on or off duty, to travel free in standard class on trains within roughly a 70 miles radius of central London, as shown by this map, upon presentation of their valid Warrant Card.

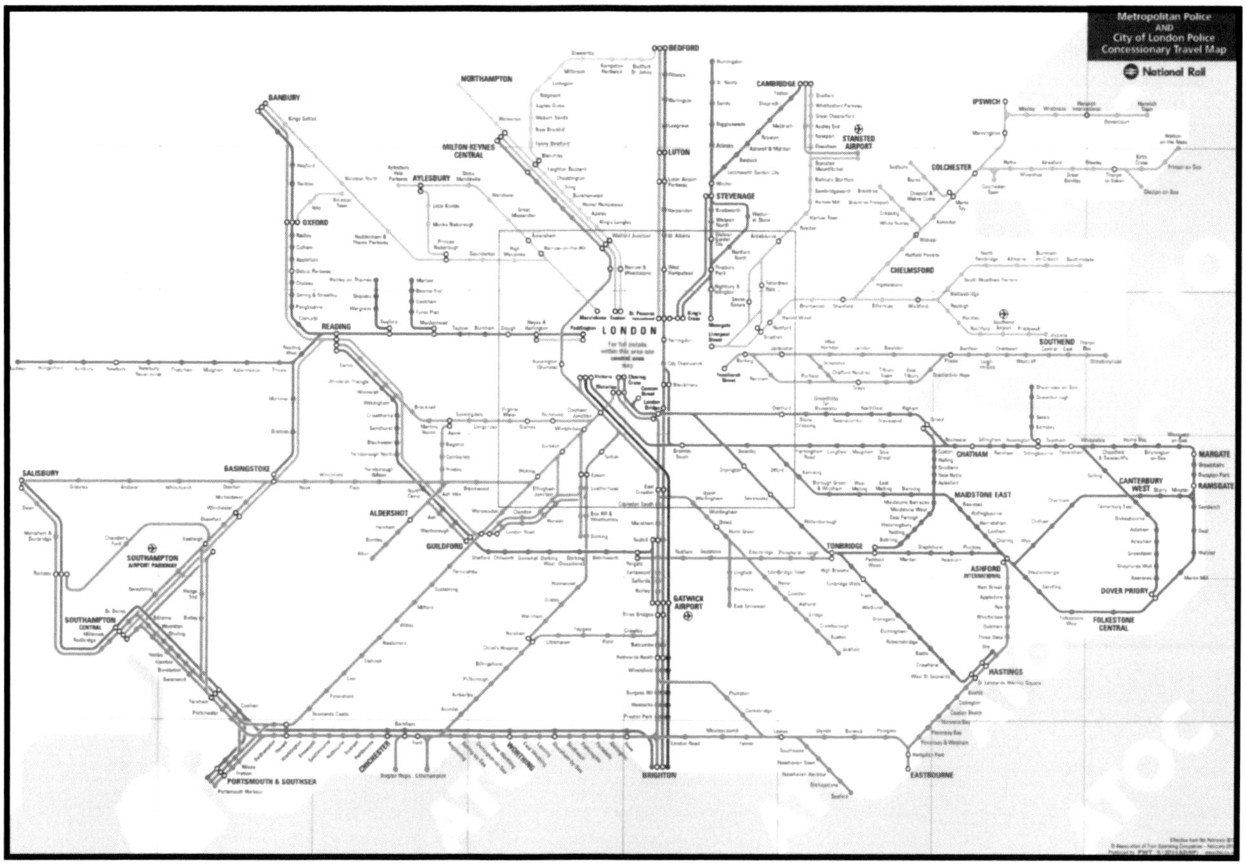


The full area is basically the old Network South Eastern area which is bounded by Salisbury; Bedwyn; Banbury; Northampton; Bedford; Huntingdon; Cambridge; Stansted; Ipswich; Harwich; Walton/Clacton; Southminster; Shoeburyness; and around the coast including Southampton back to Salisbury.

There are some exceptions to the coverage as, for example, it does not provide free travel on SouthEastern's Javelin service. It should be noted that only City of London officers who have "opted in" to the concessionary travel scheme are entitled to travel free. City of London officers who have not "opted in" are provided with a Warrant Card endorsed "Not valid for ATOC travel".

What are a brass pass and a standard card season ticket doing together? Well, the pass and the season ticket are for the same journey as York Road was renamed firstly to York Road and Battersea Park in November 1870, then secondly to Battersea Park and York Road in 1877 and finally plain Battersea Park in June 1885.

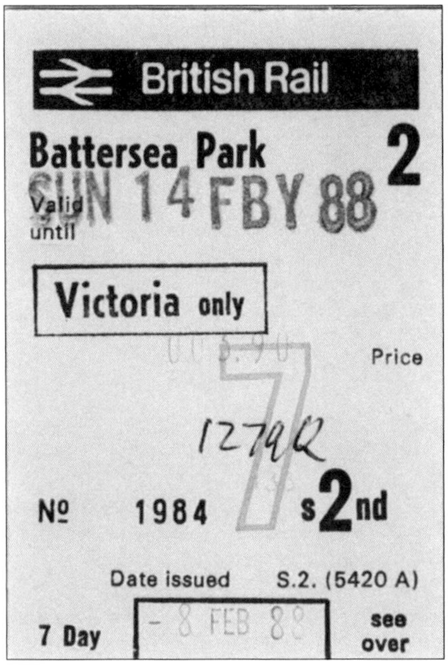


Brass is also the material for a Great Eastern Railway workman's pass between Harwich and Parkeston.

Brass is certainly not for the good commuters of Harrow On The Hill, nor of the south western suburbs, they wanted something more grand, such as enamel. Not strictly "tickets" but something that could go on a watch chain and keep the true ticket housed safely.

A couple of the true "tickets" from the 1920's

Why so many Privilege season tickets to Beckenham Junction? The railways have gone through the Grouping, Nationalisation, Network South East and Privatisation but the South Eastern Chatham & Dover, the London, Brighton and South Coast and the London & South Western, have refused to die. These seasons are from a period when the Southern Region was split into three with the South Eastern Division being run from offices at Beckenham Junction. The former offices have now been converted into flats.

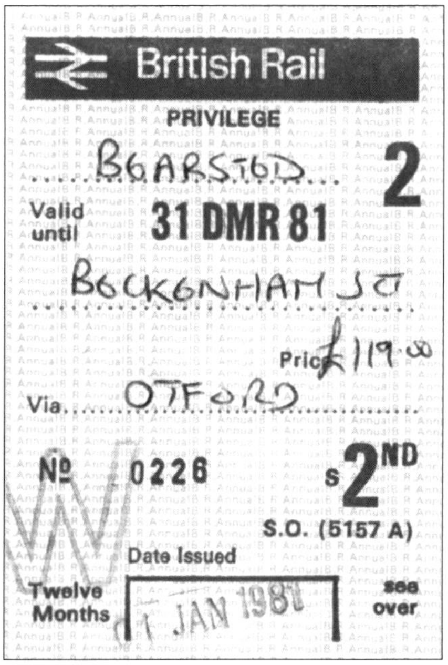


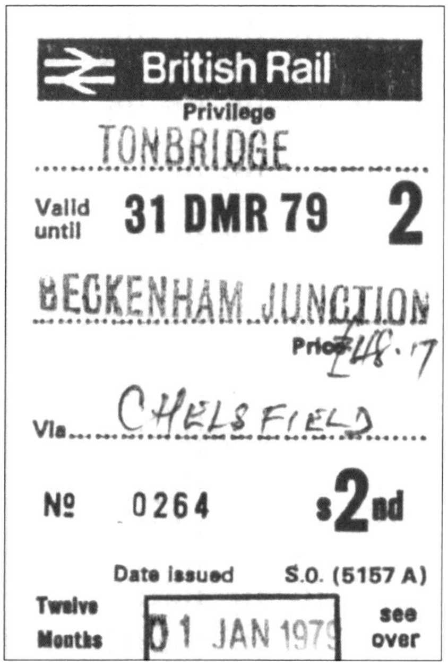

To round off, here are a few railway employee's Duty passes. The LB&SC railway one is not for "Workmen" but for "Labourers". The conditions at the bottom of the ticket are interesting requiring the pass to be given up to the Time Keeper on each arrival at Newhaven. The Railway Executive ticket is also interesting in it being for two men Employed in the Service of the Executive and leaves you in no doubt about it being a duty ticket as apart from the endorsement in red across the front of the ticket, in large letters on the back, is the condition that it not for residential purposes and not just for "workmen" but specifically for Workmen in "Workmen's Dress".

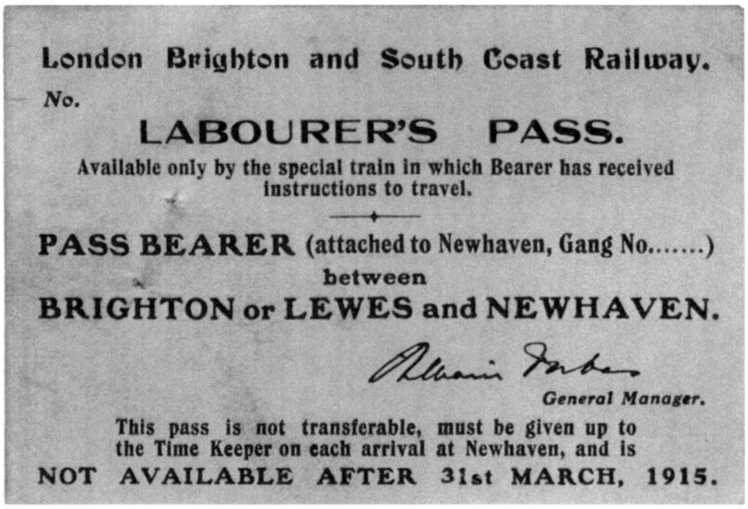

London Brighton and South Coast Railway.
No.
LABOURER'S PASS.
Available only by the special train in which Bearer has received instructions to travel.

PASS BEARER (attached to Newhaven, Gang No.......)
between
BRIGHTON or LEWES and NEWHAVEN.

General Manager.

This pass is not transferable, must be given up to the Time Keeper on each arrival at Newhaven, and is
NOT AVAILABLE AFTER 31st MARCH, 1915.

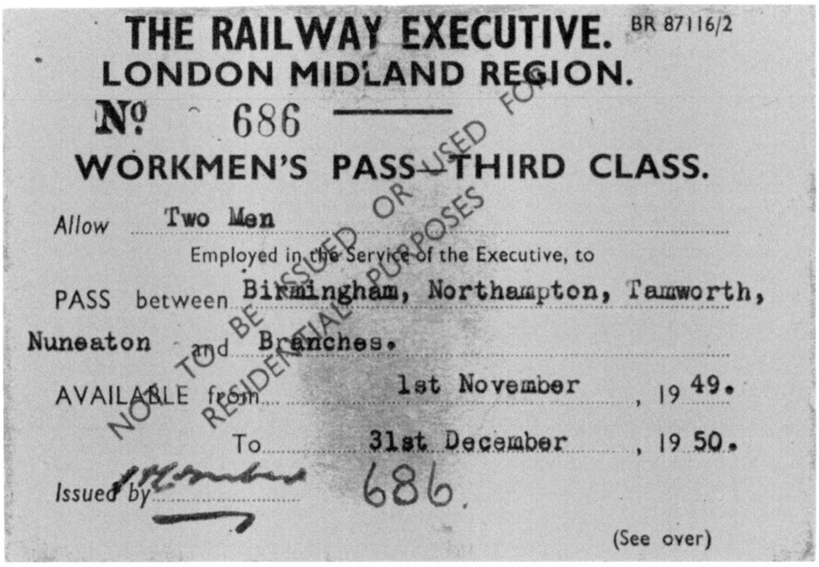

THE RAILWAY EXECUTIVE. BR 87116/2
LONDON MIDLAND REGION.
No 686
WORKMEN'S PASS—THIRD CLASS.
Allow Two Men
Employed in the Service of the Executive, to
PASS between Birmingham, Northampton, Tamworth, Nuneaton and Branches.
AVAILABLE from 1st November, 19 49.
To 31st December, 19 50.
Issued by 686.
(See over)

NOT TO BE ISSUED OR USED FOR RESIDENTIAL PURPOSES

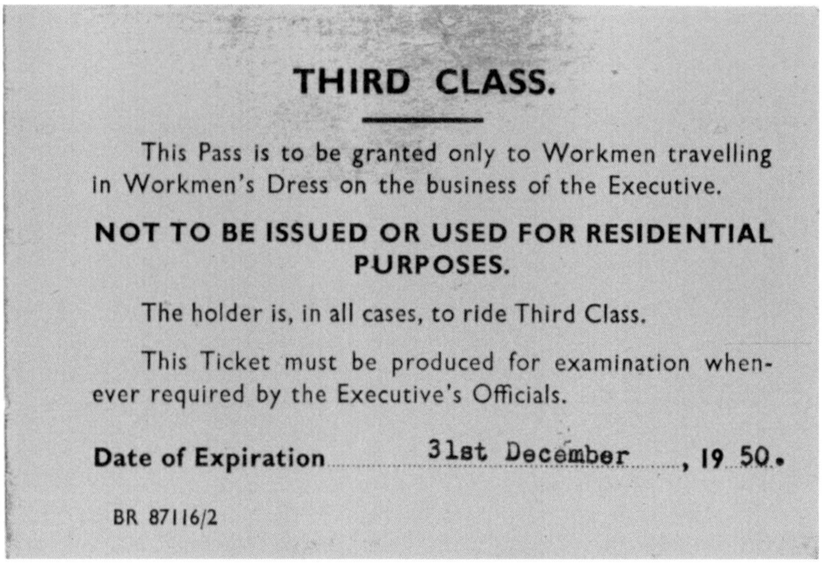

THIRD CLASS.

This Pass is to be granted only to Workmen travelling in Workmen's Dress on the business of the Executive.

NOT TO BE ISSUED OR USED FOR RESIDENTIAL PURPOSES.

The holder is, in all cases, to ride Third Class.

This Ticket must be produced for examination whenever required by the Executive's Officials.

Date of Expiration 31st December, 19 50.

BR 87116/2

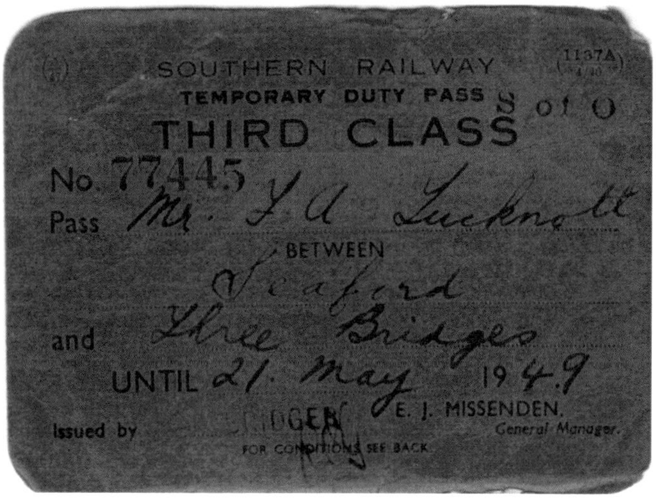
SOUTHERN RAILWAY (1137A)
TEMPORARY DUTY PASS 8 of 0
THIRD CLASS
No. 77445
Pass Mr. F A Lucknott
BETWEEN
Seaford
and Three Bridges
UNTIL 21. May 1949
Issued by ... E. J. MISSENDEN, General Manager.
FOR CONDITIONS SEE BACK

In 1910 the LB&SCR bought land in Lancing for a carriage works. There was opposition from the local population as this was a rural area at the time Because of its rural setting the railway ran a special daily train from Brighton to Lancing. By the 1960's over 1,500 workers were employed at the works. Rationalisation saw the works run down and eventually closed in 1965 despite protests this time to keep the works open.

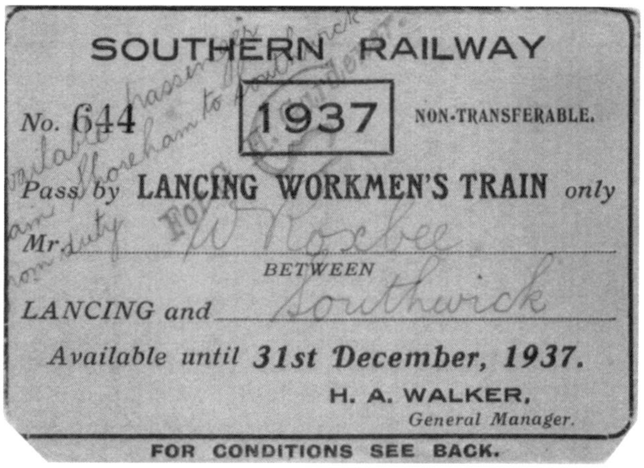
SOUTHERN RAILWAY
No. 644 1937 NON-TRANSFERABLE.
Pass by LANCING WORKMEN'S TRAIN only
Mr. W Roxbee
BETWEEN
LANCING and Southwick
Available until 31st December, 1937.
H. A. WALKER, General Manager.
FOR CONDITIONS SEE BACK.

Some of the passes are explicit about being a Duty pass or a Residential pass while others are silent on the matter other than having "R" or "L". in large capital letters. R being Residential.

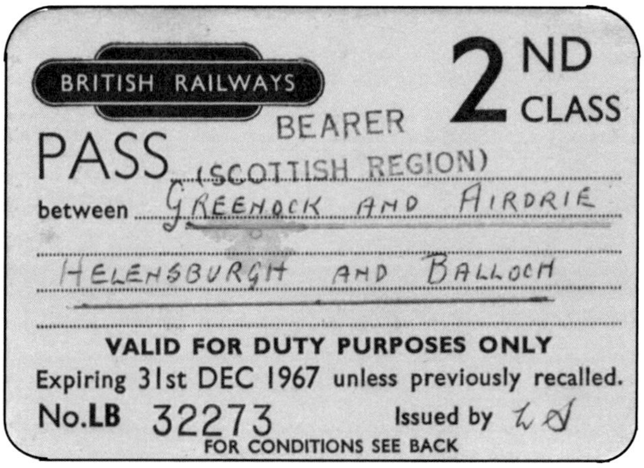
BRITISH RAILWAYS 2ND CLASS
PASS BEARER (SCOTTISH REGION)
between GREENOCK AND AIRDRIE
HELENSBURGH AND BALLOCH
VALID FOR DUTY PURPOSES ONLY
Expiring 31st DEC 1967 unless previously recalled.
No.LB 32273 Issued by
FOR CONDITIONS SEE BACK

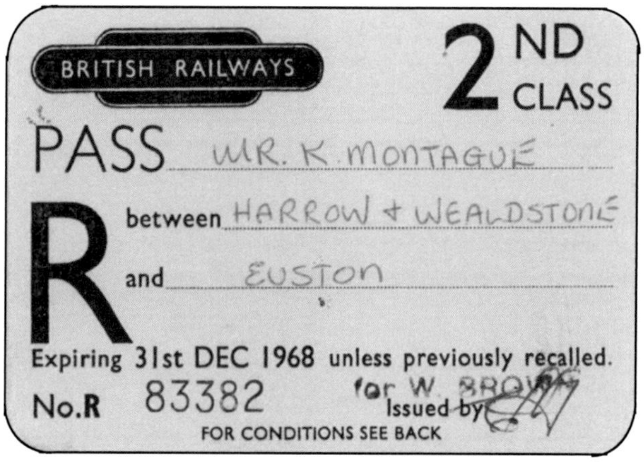
BRITISH RAILWAYS 2ND CLASS
PASS MR. K. MONTAGUE
R between HARROW & WEALDSTONE
and EUSTON
Expiring 31st DEC 1968 unless previously recalled.
No.R 83382 for W. BROWN Issued by
FOR CONDITIONS SEE BACK

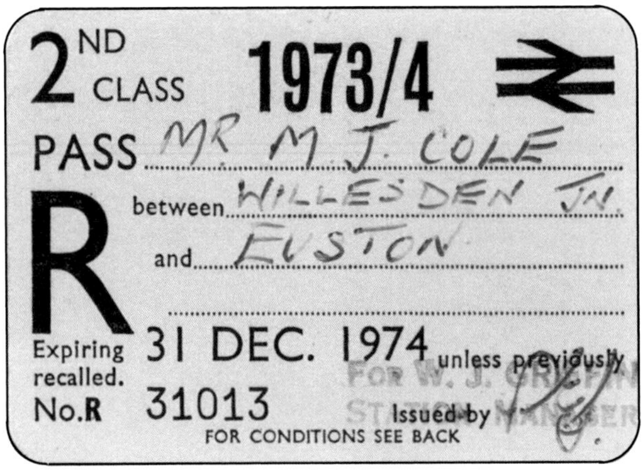

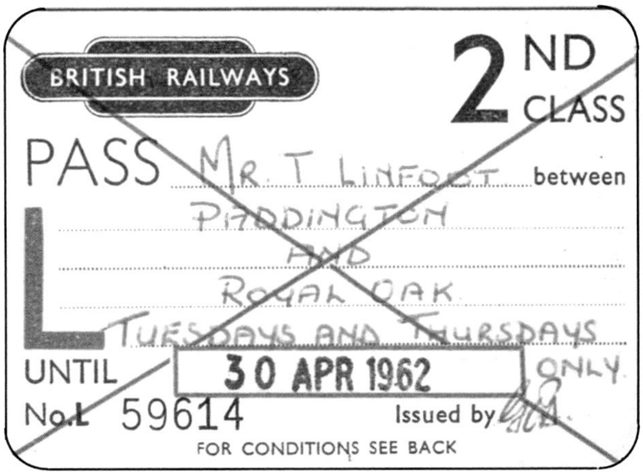


Tickets with a prominent red "L" are "Learning". This accounts for them having odd periods and day restrictions. In the bottom illustration the course or training was only held on the days specified.

Finally a little more recent. We have now reached Standard Class and post privatisation Duty Passes.

Railtrack was one of the companies that appeared with the privatisation of the railway network. There were fatal accidents at Southall and Ladbroke Grove but it was the Hatfield crash that was the beginning of the end of Railtrack. This exposed the need for expensive safety work throughout the country which, together with politics, pushed Railtrack towards insolvency. In October 2001 the company went into Railway Administration.

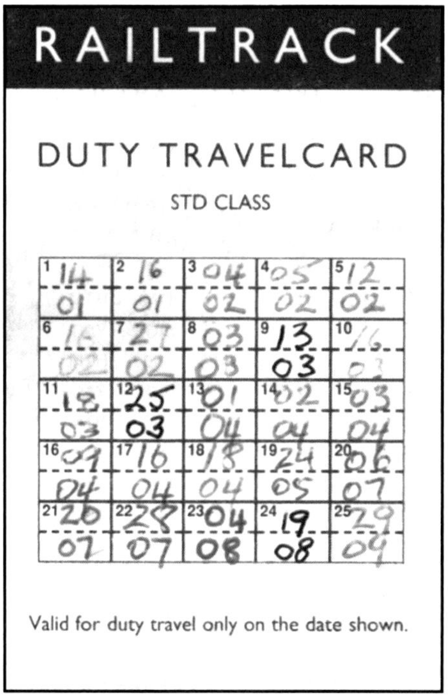


Virgin Rail Group suffered the fallout from the collapse of Railtrack. When Virgin won the Inter City West Coast franchise, Railtrack was to upgrade the West Coast Main Line to allow tilting trains to operate at 140 mph by 2005. In the wake of the collapse of Railtrack and the inability of their successors, Network Rail, to deliver on the 140 mph West Coast Main Line upgrade, both the Virgin Cross Country and Virgin West Coast franchises were suspended in favour of management contracts.

Connex South Eastern won the franchise to operate services until 2011 but on the 27th June 2003 the Strategic Rail Authority terminated the franchise citing poor financial management.

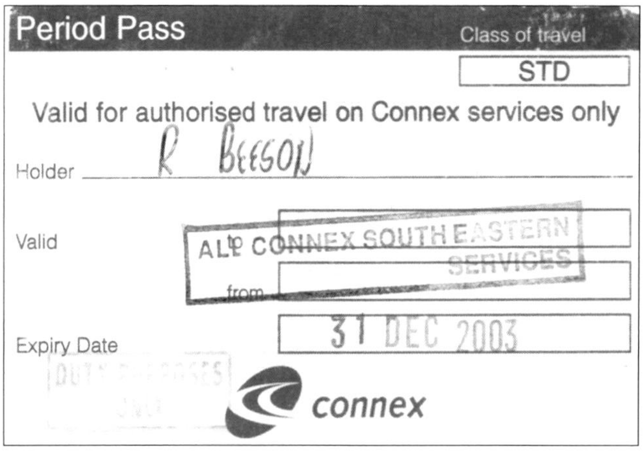


Peeping Ltd was a company that offered research services to Train Operating Companies. In July 2009 the company was bought by Tracsis Ltd. Tracsis's client base includes a majority of U.K. transport operators and also Network Rail and the government's Department for Transport.

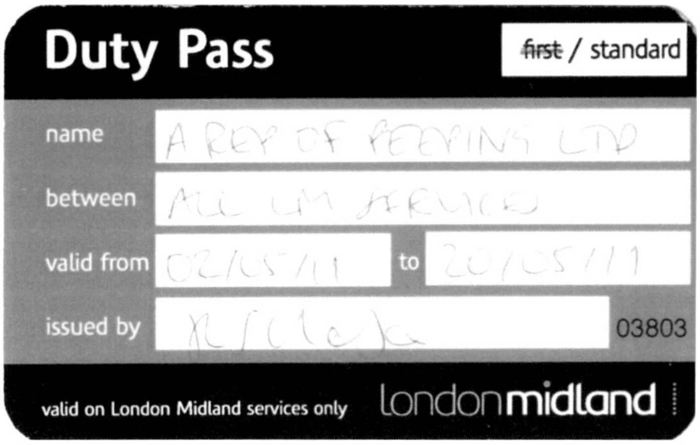

Many of the Duty Passes that are issued are for a period, quite often annual. The South Western Trains pass is just for one day. The CDP prefix to the serial number probably stands for Contractors' Duty Pass.

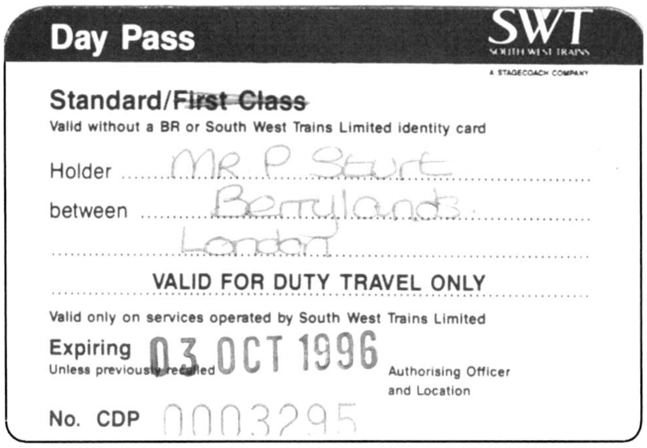
Day Pass
SWT
SOUTH WEST TRAINS
A STAGECOACH COMPANY
Standard/First Class
Valid without a BR or South West Trains Limited identity card
Holder
between
VALID FOR DUTY TRAVEL ONLY
Valid only on services operated by South West Trains Limited
Expiring 03 OCT 1996
Unless previously recalled
Authorising Officer and Location
No. CDP 0003295

What of the future? Many of the types looked at in this talk are obsolete and others are heading that way. Is the paper ticket doomed to be replaced by smart cards? Some predict that this will be achieved in 10 to 15 years. Customised period Oyster Cards were produced to enable Games Makers and other staff to travel to and from their work areas in the Olympic Park or elsewhere in London venues, free of charge provided the journey was within zones 1/6, and provided they were displaying their Games or Ceremonies accreditation.

oyster®
London Olympic Games
Issued subject to conditions – see over

oyster®
London Paralympic Games
Issued subject to conditions – see over

Travelcard
Valid only when seen with accompanying event ticket
Paralympic Games
Valid only on
Zones
29 AUG 2012 »123456789«
Number
PA057440
29081 2057440
Not for resale • Issued subject to conditions - see over

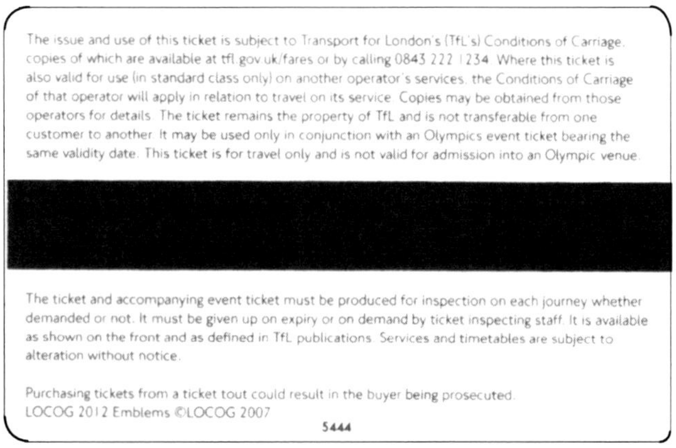
The issue and use of this ticket is subject to Transport for London's (TfL's) Conditions of Carriage, copies of which are available at tfl.gov.uk/fares or by calling 0843 222 1234. Where this ticket is also valid for use (in standard class only) on another operator's services, the Conditions of Carriage of that operator will apply in relation to travel on its service. Copies may be obtained from those operators for details. The ticket remains the property of TfL and is not transferable from one customer to another. It may be used only in conjunction with an Olympics event ticket bearing the same validity date. This ticket is for travel only and is not valid for admission into an Olympic venue.
The ticket and accompanying event ticket must be produced for inspection on each journey whether demanded or not. It must be given up on expiry or on demand by ticket inspecting staff. It is available as shown on the front and as defined in TfL publications. Services and timetables are subject to alteration without notice.
Purchasing tickets from a ticket tout could result in the buyer being prosecuted.
LOCOG 2012 Emblems ©LOCOG 2007
5444

However, the thousands of spectators were provided with paper Day Travelcards covering zones 1/9 for the date printed on their event ticket. So perhaps there is some hope for the humble paper ticket after all

We shall see!!!.

## Acknowledgements

A History of London Transport – Volume 2.
Association of Train Operating Companies
The Bristol Tramways & Carriage Company Ltd – G.E. Serpell-Morris
The Transport Ticket Society *Journal*
The People's Friend (Fisher Girls)
The Transport Ticket Society Occasional Paper No.4 (Strathclyde)
The Directory of Railway Stations – R.V.J. Butt

## Wikipedia

Adeer Works
Boer War
British Aerospace
Cement Mills Halt
Fontwell Park
HMS Ganges
Henlow Camp
Kent Coalfield
Kiveton Colliery
Knowle Mental Hospital
Lancing Carriage Works
Partition of Ireland
ROF Ranskill
Rolls Royce
Sellafield
Singer Manufacturing Company
Stanlow
Stranraer
The Tote
Wedgwood
Wellworthy

## Internet

bbc.co.uk/news (Bridgnorth)
shropshirestar.com
bbc.co.uk/history/domesday/dblock/GB-45600-108000/page/71 (Knowle)
rolls-royce.com
atoc.org
babbacombecliffrailway.co.uk
bbc.co.uk/Bristol/content/article/2005/12/23 pwaod_cigarettes_feature.s htm
bbc.co.uk/history/domesday/dblock/GB-428000-96000/page/14 (Wellworthy)
bbc.co.uk/news/world-europr-22425684 (Irish "Deserters")
gracesguide.co.uk/wellworthy
humberbridge.co.uk
ipswichstar.co.uk/1.94898 (Anglia Commuter Club)
littlehampton.org.uk
met.police.uk
newhavenferryport.co.uk
northernracing.co.uk
oblivionstate.com (Oxcroft Colliery)
oldminer.co.uk (Glapwell Colliery)
rakaia.co.uk (Alfred Holt)
singerdirect.co.uk
tracsis.com
visitstranraerandtherhins.co.uk
webspinners.org.uk (Ansley Hall)
youtube.com (Renishaw Park Colliery)